The Glory Of It All!

Sermons On The Gospel Readings For Sundays In Lent And Easter

Cycle C

Donald Charles Lacy

CSS Publishing Company, Inc., Lima, Ohio

THE GLORY OF IT ALL!

For more information about CSS Publishing Company resources, visit our website at
www.csspub.com or e-mail us at custserv@csspub.com or call (800) 241-4056.

Cover design by Barbara Spencer
ISBN 0-7880-2426-4   PRINTED IN U.S.A.

*Dedicated to the
High Street United Methodist Church
of Muncie, Indiana,
where I was baptized
and received into the church
in the spring of 1954*

Table Of Contents

Preface   7

Ash Wednesday   9
The Hard Sell
Matthew 6:1-6, 16-21

Lent 1   17
Testing Time
Luke 4:1-13

Lent 2   25
No Intimidation
Luke 13:31-35

Lent 3   33
More Time
Luke 13:1-9

Lent 4   39
The Two Prodigals
Luke 15:1-3, 11b-32

Lent 5   47
Holy Extravagance
John 12:1-8

Sunday Of The Passion/   55
Palm Sunday
(Lent 6)
History Hangs In The Balance
Luke 23:1-49

Good Friday   **63**
A Frightening Friday
John 18:1—19:42

The Resurrection Of Our Lord/   **71**
Easter Day
Mary Magdalene's Day
John 20:1-18

Easter 2   **79**
Those Who Doubt
John 20:19-31

Easter 3   **87**
Fish And Sheep
John 21:1-19

Easter 4   **95**
So, Are You The Messiah?
John 10:22-30

Easter 5   **101**
Recognizing His Disciples
John 13:31-35

Easter 6   **107**
Keeping His Word
John 14:23-29

The Ascension Of Our Lord   **113**
A Good-bye Topping All Others
Luke 24:44-53

Easter 7   **121**
Call To Oneness
John 17:20-26

Preface

What is better than preaching, writing, and listening to sermons? Well, not much! All these events are opportunities for growth given to us by the Holy Spirit. The laity and clergy across our land are very privileged.

The holy season of Lent and Easter is a remarkably glorious time for professing Christians to celebrate. In fact, without this blessed time we have a mere philosophy of life and not a victorious faith!

These sermons have all been written after calling upon the Holy Spirit. Guidance was sought that the Word of God would be presented in all its magnificence and practicality, despite the imperfections of the writer and preacher.

Prayers are given that each comes alive from the printed page. In truth, the Holy Spirit makes or breaks our sermons! Nearly fifty years of preaching have taught me we are merely instruments and/ or vehicles of God's Word.

Please read these sermons with serious joy. Preaching is a noble, spiritual art. Our faith is one which is never ultimately defeated and in our depths we know this beyond doubt. Always give thanks for the crucified and resurrected Christ.

A special word of thanks goes to Judy Marsh, an administrative secretary, committed to excellence.

Donald Charles Lacy

The Hard Sell

Our blessed Lord presses the issue. Do you or do you not want to be my disciple? If you do not, then it is with great sadness that your Savior must move on with those who are willing to fully commit themselves.

In our lives, each and every one of us receives Christ's invitation of discipline and abandonment of the world. No longer are we getting acquainted. We are being asked to come into a relationship at once glorious and painful. Yes, it comes to all of us — sooner or later.

It is like moving from an introductory offer, which we explore, and then deciding whether or not to buy into the entire program. There is a host of witnesses that function, I like to think, like a cheerleading team. They want us and plead with you and me to come into the most blessed fold of all.

There is nothing academic or even philosophical about all of this. It is more a matter of, "Do you or don't you?" — so much depends upon our answers. To avoid and evade over a period of time, perhaps years, is to say, "No." Are there regrets in this experience? You bet there are! We must be realistic.

Our Lord commands us to do that which is against our natural tendencies. After all, why shouldn't we show off our good deeds? Dear Jesus, you have called us to witness and others must see our splendid work! Surely we waste our time and energy by not displaying the giving spirit in our lives! If others don't know about these wonderful acts of discipleship, how can the world be expected to believe? Well, yes, that is you and me — at least — upon some

9

occasions. Isn't it interesting and irritating how the problem seems to recur all during our lifetimes? Some of us may even have secret diaries that resemble *Saint Augustine's Confessions*.

The world says show off your achievements. The dear Lord says do your ministries in the quietude and holy secrecy that best serves his purpose. The world says we must not hide our good deeds and the more they are seen, the better. The world says don't restrain your natural tendencies of wanting others to see and especially reward, your accomplishments. Yes, the world keeps right on insisting that we are to look at how others view our expressed goodness, even if we have to hire a publicist! But our dear Lord has other plans and they are intended for the saving of our eternal souls. Often, this is a more clear-cut choice than we would like to admit.

There are those popular philosophers and theologians who believe in the innate goodness of man. They will tell you that at birth we are totally clean and rightly motivated. Whatever we do is simply a means to enhance a goodness we have had from the very beginning. In fact, serious religion of any variety may be an obstruction to our naturally intended growth. How do we answer this? If they are right, then the Adam and Eve story has no validity. Even more importantly, the coming of a Savior to right our wrongs — indeed, forgive our sins — is mostly hogwash. Granted, our Lord's request can be a "hard sell."

In all honesty, the "back to nature" theme and method of living can have its solidly desirable and suitable points. Who can argue with the promotion of clean air and pure water? Who can seriously challenge the call to relieve us of the pollution in our lives? In an environment which raises many crucial questions, we know the truth of this rightful quest. At the same time what would the most purified environment look like without the internal and very personal cleansing of Jesus Christ? It does not seem the proponents of pristine living conditions know quite what to do with that momentous and essential inquiry. Perhaps professing Christians have not spent enough time looking at and praying for our natural surroundings. Granted, but never at Jesus' expense!

Our Lord calls us to a depth the world does not know. To be an alien in this life has become a rather popular theme and topic in recent years. Of course, this is nothing new. The New Testament apprises us of this. While living out our lives among others, we are continually reminded of this state of affairs. In short, there is a difference — even qualitative — between committed followers of Christ and those who are minimally interested or not interested at all. Those of us who listen carefully to his voice have a struggle with this and it has a lot more to do with our lives than on Ash Wednesday once each year! We must learn to be content with our "alien" status.

The Master told his disciples it would be that way. He tells you and me — sometimes frequently — that's the way it is. We are on different wavelengths. We discover that our assumptions about life and even our most cherished beliefs do not strike a significant chord with those seemingly content to live as the world directs. Our best mode of behavior is to succumb to the blessed reality, in our case, that all is well with us because we have seen a great light in the darkness. Forbid we feel superior! Forbid we overlook the necessary Christlike compassion that is a beacon to an otherwise lost and dying world. Yes, our work (ministry) is cut out for us. It is an old/new battle.

One of the dangers that strangely poses itself in taking Saint Matthew's words with supreme seriousness is the subtle temptation of "self-elevation." How often we have seen the finest and best be virtually annulled by an attitude of thinking of ourselves too highly. To be separate and distinct as holy people somehow gets translated into "I am better than you are." The devil is much at work (and play) here! His twists and turns seem never to stop, as he persistently seeks to trick us into becoming more abomination than blessing. We are never truly big enough within ourselves to handle these fabrications and machinations. The Holy Spirit must be present.

It is always wise to remember that wherever the greatest spiritual success comes into being, there is likewise the greatest opportunity for the evil one to derail the highest and best we know. Pause for a time and recollect the moments in your lives this has happened. We forget our common humanity and believe we are more than sinners saved by the grace of God! It is a slippery slope. We are called to invigorating celebration but can end up in debilitating frustration. Indeed, the vast majority of us are not called to hibernate in prayer on a faraway island. Our Lord instills within us the motivation and equips us to live out our days victoriously among other people. Some are saintly and some not so saintly! How fortunate we are.

Our Lord wants us to be "low profile" for the benefit of all. Virtually every word tells us exactly that in our text. Be a braggadocio if you must — but that is not the way of Christ. Sound the trumpets and call attention to your giving but don't label that Christ's way of doing things. Some of us have this ongoing itch to let others in on our good deeds, so they can — at least — smile with affirmation. If someone doesn't scratch it for us, we do it ourselves! Some might call this unfair and even unjust but for the moment let's be brutally honest. If we seek to stand out before others and take unlimited bows, how in the name of high heaven can we benefit anyone?

We are led by the Holy Spirit to benefit others. Why? For the simple reason that this is the behavior our Master lays before us and urges us to accept. Don't let others know you are fasting for them. If the Holy Spirit causes them to learn this precious thing is taking or has taken place, so be it. Most of us on such a journey know this happens from time to time. It is God's doing and not ours. His will and ways are always to have priority. Christ sets the pattern and we are to emulate him, come what may. So, the message is crystal clear — or is it? Again, there is this fallen nature that rears its ugly and sinister head. It says that if we do something good, others should know.

You may say, "But, pastor, we all have the need to be praised by others." If that is our basic motivation, then as the scripture says — we have received our reward. How can we possibly serve others by constantly demanding attention and thanks in our own ways? The answer to that is obvious. We can't. Among our cumulative experiences, there must be dozens and even hundreds of good people we have known who insist on being given credit for their good deeds, monetary or otherwise. Really, is it praise or sincere affirmation from others we need? Ponder that for a time and you will see the chasm separating the two. The most affirming person in the universe is our Lord!

Treasures on earth are often summed up in property and money. We can't seem to keep from putting price tags on everyone and everything. Who and what are you to a world that is immersed in such a mentality? We even put a monetary sticker on those in our sacred ordained ministry! Just maybe, on judgment day our Lord will implement "the last shall be first and the first shall be last"! Then, the worldly label of dollar bills on each head will run amuck and he will have a free-for-all on his hands because we could never think in any other way. Perhaps we will then come begging to enter the heavenly gates, being freed from our secular mindset. Is this an excursion into a fanciful and unrealistic world? Frankly, that is doubtful and it is time for clergy to confess.

Our Lord gives a glimpse of where lasting riches are. It comes down to a choice, doesn't it? If we but look carefully at our passage of holy scripture, the obvious is before us. If we choose to play psychological games and attempt to rationalize our human nature into something of pure beauty, we have missed this lofty Ash Wednesday message. As we know, such a choice is continually before us. It is not a matter of a one-time answer set in cement. If we fail to get it the first time, it is still there. Even if we fail many times, it is in the recesses of our souls. To have once received and implemented it is no guarantee we live by its wisdom.

Every so-called secular or worldly accomplishment in our world can be taken from us. Who knows the amount of money, time, and energy that goes into the print or other media to explain away someone's good deeds? Those sorts of shenanigans appear to go on all the time. The calculated deceit in today's world stretches our imaginations! Only what we have done for Christ and consequently stored up in heaven is free from such onslaughts. It is a simple, spiritual truth but human nature is often hell-bent on discrediting it. Our saved souls yearn for permanent treasures. Only by living Christ's ways can they be there at our death.

If we place our hearts in this world's treasures, we have a big problem. It is going to evaporate or worse! The titans of today and the past have all had to deal with it. The little folks, like you and me, also have to deal with it. We can condemn such people and even — in our own minds — send them to hell, but that by no means indicates that they are going there. Some of us have laid up treasures in heaven and we are not so concerned about who has the biggest treasure, but that what we do have is safe and secure. Yes, that is the way it is for those of us, who in our many sins of omission and commission, have sought to conquer, with the Holy Spirit's full assistance, our fallen nature.

To trust any human being totally and completely — almost without exception — is a big mistake, perhaps catastrophic. Not to trust God totally and completely is a mistake we cannot afford to make. If he is wrong, there is no hope for anyone. If he is right through his Son, Jesus Christ — and he always is — even our lowly common sense tells us to pay close attention! To be sure, we are in an arena taxing our hearts and minds. Our perceptions and perspectives can be outlandishly wrong. But we certainly do have a glimpse, don't we? We are not blind beggars with no shepherd and physician. The Holy Spirit is among us and the law of the Savior's love pursues us, seeking our healing submission.

At the beginning of Lent, it is time to move beyond our convenient and well-accepted Christian practice. It is time to move boldly (or humbly) away from showing others we belong to Christ and to please watch what we do! Away with worship attendance mostly to be seen. Away with prayers having more to do with others hearing our perfectly spoken words. Away with giving all of our money in checks, so there is an accurate record for the church and the IRS. Away with ushering and greeting to show we are active in the church. Bring on the anonymity for which our blessed Lord calls! Bring on the blessedness wrought by not letting the left hand know what the right hand is doing!

The world has an ongoing lust for security. How can we keep our stocks and bonds from slipping away from us? How can we keep our popularity and have others always think well of us? How can we secure a place for ourselves in history forever and ever? In all cases, we are living in quicksand, which may devour us at any-time and most any place. As committed Christians, we know our treasures can be sealed in heaven, where neither moth nor rust consumes. We also know our treasures can be safe, where thieves do not break in and steal. It is a call for tears of joy because we have found the "pearl of great price." The Lord holds our treasures and will present them to us on that great day!

Testing Time

To live the Christian life is to be tested. As day follows night and night follows day, we experience it all of our days. The deeper we go, the more testing comes upon us. So, there is nothing unique about all of this. If we expect our daily walk with Christ to be any different, we are guilty of self-deception.

Sometimes it is really severe and we wonder about its cessation. Patience becomes virtually non-existent. Strength seems to go out the window and we languish not only in pain but borderline disillusionment. They are not fun times! The sooner such episodes go on their way, we are greatly relieved.

As we attempt to survey the ages of church history, aren't we strengthened to know there are many similar experiences? It is our common lot but let us not be content to stop there. It is not only Christians who face these times, all of humanity finds it omnipresent. That is the way it is!

Before we begin on a non-productive negative binge, let's recount the times our testing has led to blessings untold. Our Lord has not abandoned us and, in fact, he makes a point of reminding us of the harshness of his own testing that came upon him as God's earthly Son.

Are we able to live by bread alone? To live in this world is to be engulfed in the material side of it. To be hungry is to be hungry! Yes, our dear Lord must have been famished. It would not take nearly forty days for you and me to reach that stage. Could we even go one week or ten days? In the depths of our souls we have, at least, some answers. It sure would be "tough stuff." Imagine all of the hunger pangs to be experienced. Visualize all the days of good cooking that we could not enjoy. It begins to be not only a potentially inconvenient experience, but one of honest-to-goodness discomfort.

We know what our Lord's point is, don't we? He wants us to shift our fixation on "bread and potatoes" to something that transcends the necessities of this world. Come on now, disciple, let's get serious about things beyond our favorite restaurants and church dinners. Granted, the food industry seemingly at every turn tries to persuade us it's time to eat or drink. Do you get the idea we are expected to get up eating and drinking and retire at night still filling our mouths? Maybe it is not quite that bad but expand it to include an array of things we are supposed to purchase. Advertising can be so disarming. The devil can be so slick and not be close to a wilderness.

Some decidedly spiritual souls have learned that the more they deny themselves of food and drink, the more they sense the closeness of Jesus, their Christ. Those who have gone to their beds from sheer exhaustion must truly be receiving accolades in heaven. The stories are many and reliable sources convey to us their validity. Church history is punctuated by those dear and precious ones who know firsthand the truthful reality our Master presents. Praise God for these jewels who keep on sparkling in our midst! What is the secret to their impact? They simply and responsibly have taken the Man of Galilee seriously. Are you and I among them? What has the Holy Spirit said to you about this?

The materialism of America is widely — yes, universally — known. For all of our goodness and attempted good deeds, there is a shadow bringing question marks. Perhaps, underlying our witness is the fear of not living by bread alone. Our lives have become so saturated by consumerism, we are hardly able to think outside of such a mentality. The late Pope John Paul II spoke to our spiritual deficiency charitably but firmly. Like most instances, we need to pay attention to his teachings — both Catholic and non-Catholic. Being familiar with actual deprivation and practicing holy disciplines, his message is of one healing our depths and not our surfaces. Our automobiles, homes, clothes, food, and drink are no substitutes for something far more precious.

Are we able to live without worldly power? Isn't power downright fascinating? It cuts across every segment of society and finds its way into even the most humble situations. Every pastor — after some years in the ministry — knows he/she does not have any real choice; it is built into the fabric of who and what we are. To refuse to deal with it is to deal with it in ways not likely to be fruitful. The finest people in our churches, rightly motivated, deal with it. When they are mature and spiritually oriented, they are great assets to pastors. They can make potentially disastrous situations turn into things of great beauty.

But remember, Jesus was promised all the kingdoms of the world, provided he worshiped the devil. It is also wise for you and me to remember that the devil is not likely to promise us nearly as much! Yet, the temptation to the wrong kind of power or the exercise of it is much with us. Never underestimate the evil in our midst; it comes to us in forms of goodness but, in reality, demonic excesses are waiting to destroy. To believe we can escape the sly and usually hidden agendas of evil is to be guilty of self-deception. Our Achilles' heel is often over something or someone, seemingly insignificant. Is there paranoia at work? Maybe. However, just because we are paranoid doesn't mean the devil isn't after us!

The rightful exercise of power is what the world always needs and — to be sure — what our churches always need. The devil was coming at our Lord for all the wrong reasons. To be brief, our Lord was pressured to back away from his calling and become an earthly dictator. Don't the lowly like you and I discover that likewise this can be our plight? As long as we sell our souls to Satan, we can have power in abundance for our own exaltation. You want control over the official board or trustees — the devil can make it happen! Is that overstating our case? Perhaps — but don't deny that we often teach the concept of unconditional acceptance. The church could do so much good — if I had complete control of the board!

There is such a mixing of worldly and spiritual power, it's hard to know the difference. Our answer to the quandary is found in abandonment to the Holy Spirit. The scriptures tell us that as our sure and certain guide. As we give ourselves, pastor and people, to the Lord without conditions attached, good and evil begin to separate before our Spirit-infused eyes. It is not for us to know all the whereofs and wherefores. It is humbling, but always true, you and I cannot know everything there is to know about people, places, and things! Our love can be "patient and kind" but that does not mean we know all the details of any situation. Our love can be free of arrogance and rudeness, but that does not mean we are filled with genius.

Are we able to live in the absence of physical miracles? If we are sons and daughters of the living God, why don't we just test him by showing unbelievers that we shall be miraculously rescued? Maybe we could make a trip to the Sears Tower and announce in advance we are going to jump from more than 100 stories. Then, we will be quick to point out that God always comes to the aid of his children. The angels will drop from the heavens and we will be unscathed. Does that sound like the beginning of a profitable Hollywood movie? Well, it is a way of putting you and me — to some extent — in Jesus' place. Maybe we should have picked out the very top of the tallest spire at one of the world's great cathedrals.

Indeed, it is testing time for that Jewish fellow barely into his ministry. As usual, the devil is crafty and insinuates that it's time the Son of God prove to the world that no one can hurt him. This could turn out to be quite a media event! It could even be promoted in such a way that gamblers would have their odds and people across the globe would have their eyes glued to the tubes. Human nature is drawn to physical miracles. We like it right there before our eyes. If Jesus takes the bait, then his Father will certainly see to it that he is not crushed and — in fact — not even scratched. It is a melodramatic scene and some still ponder, "What if Jesus had tried it?"

We have all known those precious people who seem to be waiting on a sign from heaven that involves a physical miracle. It is never enough to note and appreciate two people who formerly hated one another now loving one another. This is the wrong kind of miracle and doesn't sell much! They will insist the real test, where Christians must succeed, is physical especially before crowds who can attest to authenticity. The folks in Jesus' time were much like that. You are God's Son, well, that's fine; now let's see you perform and, if you are successful, we will believe. Credibility is always necessary in these matters. Flamboyance is not. Showing off one's special relationship to God that can even manipulate, my friends, is a bit too much.

Faith healers always seem to be — sooner or later — a mixed bag. Maybe we want them to perform so desperately, we will cut some corners to prove physical miracles. In the name of God, pray to him that is not the case! "With God all things are possible" is so hopeful and many of us believe just that. Yet, as the saying goes, "Not all things are prudent." God's will is invariably the best and fruitful in ways we can only imagine. While the holy scriptures speak of great changes physically in certain passages, this was true only in a few cases. Thousands received ministry but, apparently, only a few were healed in a physical way. Only God knows for sure.

Are we able to live in continual watchfulness? Note that the devil has finished every test and departs but only until an opportune time. That's ominous and even scary! Saint Luke makes it quite clear: The great deceiver is not at all finished. Imagine the trash talk that Jesus heard and most likely during his most trying moments. The underlying message is present and it speaks volumes about our blessed Lord's authenticity: He was a human being tested, only more so, so no one could prove he was merely going through the actions. If he had been solely fabricating his temptations how could he even remotely be considered the Savior? If the devil was programmed not to win, have we been dealt a crooked hand?

Where the most significant and relevant point comes into play is in our willingness to be watchful at all times. Lent teaches us many wonderful and most helpful things and certainly this is one of them. It's a good and marvelous state of affairs to be happy in the Lord. It is also a required attitude of heart and mind to know that such bliss is never all the time; days (and nights) of temptation and testing are sure to come. Will we be ready? It mostly depends upon our spiritual adaptability. We never assume Satan is through testing us. Our best assumption is that he will be back again and again.

But how do we keep from falling prey to incessantly looking under rocks and behind doors? Who can be ready for the guy who has been deceiving precious people since the beginning of time? Those are questions that must be asked. They are deeply spiritual, regardless of how they are phrased. The host of witnesses and those now living on this earth help us. They have traveled and are traveling the road. Have you and I been tempted more than anyone else? Are we being picked on? Why is it that some days the devil is a lot closer than God? Yes, most of us know the feeling and it doesn't do much for our self-image!

The good book tells us the fruit of the Spirit includes faithfulness, humility, and self-control. Now, we are onto how we can live a victorious Christian life and deal with temptations of various sorts day in and day out. "All things are possible with God" is not a cliché we bring out and brag about periodically. There is a harmony with the Holy Spirit which makes this true beyond all doubts. We are not losers, except in the world's sight, going to and fro wondering about God's presence. The only sure thing in life (and death) is the Father, Son, and Holy Spirit. All else pales in insignificance and eventual powerlessness. Tell the devil he can't have you. But be sure you do so by telling him God makes this possible and you don't. To know our acquired spiritual strength is to become weak ... and honest.

Three temptations that are a part of our spiritual memories need to be re-evaluated and studied to aid us in our walk with the Lord. At each juncture the testing is a grave matter. The devil is attempting to come at him at his greatest vulnerability. Does he need — desperately so — food and drink? Yes. Does he need to show the world — as the Jewish Messiah — the kingdoms all belong to him because he is God's Son? One could certainly make a case for that. Does he need to do something spectacular, especially of a physical nature, to illustrate control over the laws the Father had originally set in place? Well, that would help his case in the eyes of a lot of searching human beings.

Regardless of the persistent poignancy of our Lord's time of rough and tough testing, the experience comes down to you and me. What have we learned from his horrendous battle with the enemy of every person? As we prepare to celebrate the resurrection of the Christ, Lent becomes that fertile period of self-denial — perhaps of temptations of our own choosing. Ours is a costly discipleship that says we shall not be defeated by the one who would delight in sending us to hell. The purpose of testing is to make us spiritually strong and steadfast. Praises be to God we are his people and he will be with us in all our trials and tribulations. Count it a privilege to experience them!

No Intimidation

Boldness is necessary to accomplish ministry, especially that which is prophetic and points to judgment. Our dear Lord is boldly assertive and wants there to be no doubt about what his Father has sent him to accomplish. He provides both a lesson and model for us.

Our timidity in the face of odds is not becoming to those who profess to follow Christ. Only when it covers a determined soul for the faith is it in keeping with our commitment. Let's face it, some of the most timid souls in church can be downright raucous at athletic events!

We are called always to learn from the Man of Galilee and sometimes that is among the most simple style of living. He was not a milquetoast kind of guy! All of his heart, mind, soul, and strength were set in motion to fulfill his destiny, as directed by his Father in heaven.

If we are looking for fearless leadership, we have found it. He is daring and will not be denied. Some of us would like to see ourselves cut from that fabric and, praise God, sometimes we see miracles happen. The grace of God is allowed to work and a powerful love becomes there for all to view.

It was a time of poking serious fun at Herod Antipas. A pastor taught me long ago nothing succeeds quite like well-placed and intense humor. There is a real art to this strategy of ministry. One who is not skilled in this area and out of step with the Holy Spirit most likely will find he/she is on the agenda to be ousted! Acquiring such a method, hopefully on your knees, is truly valuable. We are prevented from becoming doormats for a good reason. If your superior wants you to rethink your style and, perhaps, crawl back to the parsonage or rectory in submission, simply point to Jesus' precedent.

In a way, it is somewhat out of character for our Lord. From one point of view, it looks like Herod is being unnecessarily baited, even negatively provoked, but that may be a way of backing away from a style that causes great discomfort. Some will quickly say that people have enough frustration in this world and why cause them any more? Well, we can be apologetic and even appeasing without initially recognizing it for what it is. Frequently, blunt honesty is what it takes in a world caught up in half-truths and outright lies. Praise be to our Savior and Lord, we don't have to be buried in a casket before our time.

There is the temptation to be a "smart mouth" and tell people off. That's why maturity and the guidance of the Holy Spirit are mandatory. We have all known those who have used the technique to tell off our enemies and ridicule them, even in public. Doing this deed may make you feel better for the moment, but what about tomorrow, even a year from now? There is a saying in some of our denominations: We had better watch what we say to a colleague; he/she may turn out to be our boss. Some of us who have been around a long time have seen exactly that happen. What does all of this do for Christ and the church?

We can't help but admire the way our Lord gets in the face of some of the Pharisees, as well as Herod. Are we willing to take that admiration and implement it, separate and apart from our preconceived agendas and outright prejudices? So much depends on how close Christ is to us and whether or not we are willing to be obedient. His expectations and ours may be something quite different. At any rate, there is nothing quite like throwing down the gauntlet in the face of those who would cause our ministries to falter or much worse. How much goes unaccomplished because we simply are not bold! There is no good reason to complicate the matter. We serve a risen Lord whose forthrightness always challenges. Aren't we fortunate?

It is a moment of putting well-meaning Pharisees in their place. As some thinkers have indicated in recent years, the Pharisees were much misunderstood. It seems, until current scholarship came along, we didn't know there was more than one kind or variety. For centuries, there was the general acceptance of their hypocrisy and strong opposition to Jesus. While we cannot know for sure their motives in warning him, we can't but wonder just maybe it was out of the goodness of their hearts they did not want to see him seriously injured or killed. We have learned to be "pharisaic" but that does not of necessity point to odious self-righteousness.

Whether they actually took Jesus' message or not, remains an open question. What we most significantly know is his answer to those who appear to be protective. He was not going to be intimidated. He gave them understanding in a language which could not be misunderstood there was no way "that fox" was going to get in the way of his mission. If he did and in a way he did, then he best know the "Jesus express" would, nevertheless, be on schedule and accomplish its purpose. Thereby, the influence of these Pharisees would not be one allowing for retreat of the Son of God. We might conjecture as to what would have happened had he listened to them and sought a more diplomatic approach.

Don't we have to do the same thing Jesus did? Aren't there times that well-meaning people have to be put in their place in order for us to get our work done? If pastors blink in some circumstances, they may very well lose their credibility. If pastors pander to those who want them to avoid conflict at all cost, have they not compromised their ministries? Granted, some are confrontational and angry enough to shoot off a cannon to kill a horsefly. Such pastors usually need time away on a regular basis for solitude and regaining perspective. Yes, those of us who have been around for many years know what this is all about! We must be certain we are attuned to the Holy Spirit.

We are counseled by the Holy Spirit to be very careful differentiating between our Lord's dictates and our personal, questionable agendas. Human nature can tell us to call down fire from heaven on most anyone who disagrees with us! That layman/laywoman trying to run the church might be sincerely looking out for every-one concerned. So, it is often a delicate matter and one that bears our best-inspired judgment. Perhaps pastoring churches, like no other calling, tests our quality of compassion and strength of deci-sion making. It seems some pastors are invariably in trouble in their parishes and for the right reasons. In my experience, in-depth growth in the parish is sooner or later closely related to our unwill-ingness to be intimidated.

It was a prophetic declaration of what was to come. Our Lord was not trying to slip up on anyone! It was as though he was point-ing out, "Here it is, folks. Pay attention to what I am saying be-cause this is the way it is going to be. You may not believe it or be able to fill in the blank spaces, but this is the way it is going to be." If you are like me, that draws upon the deepest resources in my soul and produces respect for him par excellence. We worship a Lord who is mystical by his very nature but not esoterically re-moved from us. While we must not make the error of reducing him to our levels, likewise we must not push him so far into the clouds that we lose touch.

What an incomparable faith we have! It absolutely refuses to be intimidated and put on a level where compromises crowd out its essential nature. Of course, this is what we learn or relearn during the purifying and nourishing season of Lent. In a sense, today we appear to be returning to the ancient world with its countless num-bers of gods and goddesses. All about us are major religions that have broken into numerous facets and — perhaps more importantly — pagan systems and behaviors across the globe. The number of Protestant denominations no longer has a monopoly on this! Yet, towering above it all there is the revelation of our Savior and Lord who told the world 2,000 years ago what he was going to do and then he did it.

The field of prophecy is an area of study, at least for one vet-eran pastor, remaining something of an enigma. Who knows the precious people who have been led astray by those on an ego trip contrived by Satan or disastrously, innocently wrong? Intimida-tion almost always seems to have a part in a sometimes-gross mon-ster, spiritually killing and maiming. When it comes to this field, we are nudged to keep in mind that even Jesus admits only his Father knows when the Second Coming will occur. Praise God from whom all blessings flow Jesus the Christ reveals to us all we need. His ministry was announced and consummated. We are not among the most privileged people — we *are* the most privileged people!

Jesus is set on finishing his work or ministry. Are we set on finishing ours? It is an inquiry of colossal proportions. It speaks to our destiny and the understanding of it. We may not like it, but we have it before us in some form every day of our lives. When we come into a right relationship with the Father through his Son, Jesus Christ, our needed workload begins to unfold. We are shown directions, aspects, and categories on the horizon. As Saint Paul learned, we do not see them always clearly and distinctly — if ever. We are to finish well and that means spiritual success abounding in great joy. The Lamb of God who takes away the sins of the world grants us mercy and then lasting peace.

It is a death knell for those whose rejection is generations old. The disclosure of disclosures comes before the world for all to behold. First it comes to the Jewish people — God's chosen people. It begins the gathering of pulling his people together. It is as though a hen is gathering her brood under her wings and there are the reluctant chicks who refuse to come all the way. The fight against what is intended for them is underway and continues to this very moment. Many Gentiles find their way and join the blessed congregation of the redeemed. His own people rejected him and, to a large extent, do so even now. The picture is that of God Almighty dutifully beckoning his children to come home and they refuse.

Let us not become borderline anti-Jewish and bewail their missed opportunities. We have enough to do to handle our own! Generation after generation has had witnesses for much of the world. Indeed, there have been and are innumerable disciples of the Christ — imperfect though they be — who have paraded their Christian virtues before our very eyes. Some keep wondering when the Jews by and large are going to accept their Messiah. This is God's business! When are we going to receive our Messiah with completeness and finality? Such an inquiry is placed squarely before us. We all have families in which the rejection is generations old and growing. Lent calls us to take inventory.

"Blessed is the one who comes in the name of the Lord." We knew him by way of the blessed Virgin Mary, John the Baptist, his apostles, crucifixion, and resurrection. Each segment is there for you and me to study. Each is there also for our gratitude and ongoing direction. It seems that if we have missed something or someone essential, it is our fault. Our belligerence and pride are present in ways that should humble us, bringing to us the probability of salvation. What shall a man or woman present in exchange for his/her soul? So, our Lord was not intimidated; therefore, why should we be? These are superb questions during the challenging days before crucifixion/resurrection!

Rejection is such a nasty word. We deal with it on racial, ethnic, gender, social, and political bases. It is a universal trait to be recognized: No one wants to be rejected. Then, cutting across all these categories and more, too, we discover rearing its ugly head is the rejection of Jesus Christ. This is the supreme refusal! But, dear friends, it does not have to be that way. In our depths, we know it does not have to be that way. Again and again, far too many times to count, our Savior and Lord calls and woos us to come to him and, in time, enjoy eternity with him. He finished his work centuries ago and it is there for all to see. Is there a justifiable reason to die without him? If there is, please share it with some of us!

Our Lord would not be run over by the political boss in the area. You can be sure Herod Antipas sought only to hurt, compromise, or kill him. How refreshing and brave for our hero to stand up to him, indicating he was on a mission and no one was going to stop him. Our Lord was meek and mild in some ways but never one to back away from his mission, which meant the horrors of the cross. He is the standard whereby you and I are measured. Are we willing to die for others, especially those we don't even know? He was obedient to the very end. Placed before us is a gargantuan order of bravery and courage.

It is said many times and places that everyone has a price. In other words, we can be intimidated in the right situation by the right person. Well, that includes you and me! Often this comes about by threats to our families, specifically our spouses and children. Every married pastor knows the reality of such a state of affairs in the parishes. We can be pushed in different directions because our loved ones will suffer — if we don't knuckle under. A devout person said that's the best case for celibacy! Give that suggestion some thought and be reminded as the Holy Spirit blows wherever it chooses, perhaps in our day and time even more so, we must be open to forms of ministry never thought viable. It is truly a great day to do ministry!

More Time

Who can speak of "justice" in any long-standing and helpful way? It is a subject that fits many who write commentaries but we discover in most cases they are woefully inadequate. You and I, lay and clergy, deal with it almost daily and much of the time when we would rather not do so.

It is a theme seemingly as old as history itself. Indeed, when did we not speak and write about it? The Old Testament (Hebrew Scripture) has numerous references to our topic. In that classic verse of Micah, he reminds us "to do justice." Our civilization has been much influenced by the Judeo-Christian viewpoints.

Our legal systems, both civil and religious, provide ways of knowing what is expected of us in behavior. The scales, sooner or later, are always there to do the weighing. In recent years it seems religious courts have become more important. After all, it is a trying time of sorting out the guilty and innocent.

While our preaching may seek to avoid or limit it, we discover that is hardly the case. Our intentions are aboveboard but the reality of living causes our concerns to come into the picture. So we do the best we possibly can.

Fortunately, justice was, is, and shall be in God's hands. There is a safety net here, isn't there? To classify those who are worse sinners than others or decide who has had enough time to be fruitful ultimately is in the Almighty's hands and not ours. For many of us such truth is consoling and gives us reason to look at today and the future both humbly and positively. Sometimes during periods of special stress, we are summoned in love to become patient and wait on God. How good this truly is! How difficult it may turn out to be! In these relationships we can gain strength.

Jesus warns us over and over again not to be judgmental. For one thing, he points out our utter lack of ability. For another, it poisons the people of stature, who can at times forget their relationship to God and others. In brief, we can be rightly motivated and still not get the message. How often we have experienced this in the life of the church! Assessing fines in parishes may not help us at all in regard to calling where God wants us to go, however, not to apply church discipline can be more than scandalous; it may very well be hypocritically disgraceful. Wow, what a can of odious worms we can open.

You and I need to know and openly admit that God sees our frailty and inadequacy. The concept we are speaking of tends to land us, at least, on two different sides. Perhaps, we wish with all our hearts that was not so but it certainly is. There are situations when the sides are so many, we can end up in a kind of nihilism. Nevertheless, this is our lot for the world in which we live.

Can you think of a time when you did not want God in charge of justice? Probably, we all can and that is when it involves a loved one or some figure in whom we have great confidence. Our salvation, so to speak, is found in remembering God has no beginning or end. He always has been and always will be. So, justice at the moment may be seen in time as either good or bad. But, as the saying goes "don't move to judgment too soon." Only our Creator and Redeemer has the wherewithal to handle such a heavy and complicated matter. Fairness is what God says it is. It may not appear so, but try peeking into the next century and the one after that. Remember, oh man and woman, you are dust and to dust you shall return!

Mercifully, we have today to remedy a faulty relationship with God. These words are another way of saying, "Today is the day of salvation." If this has become a cliché, it is a very good one. We have learned in our day and time how important relationships are. We may have even gone overboard in elevating the necessity of human interaction. If that is the case, we still have a lot of work to do in relationship with the Father, Son, and Holy Spirit! Mind you, these are not three gods but one perfectly united and working in total harmony. Grant we would never be confused in this classic understanding of who and what God is.

So, how is it in our relationship with God? It is an inquiry always on the table. Why? Because our entire lives and deaths are directly linked to it. There may not be tomorrow but there is always today. The finest people I have known have patterned their spiritual goings and comings in this context. They followed our blessed Lord's advice to let tomorrow take care of tomorrow. There is an undeniable and always urgent closeness here. There may or may not be opportunities to straighten out our relationship to God in the hereafter. While the ancient church, along with some of our Christian friends believe so, there is pause for all of us. If the opportunity is here, why wait? According to reputable teachers, spurning the Holy Spirit is unforgivable.

Attempt to count the times the Spirit of the living God is present, urging us to make peace with him who is all and in all. Grant mercy to us, oh, God, and we beg of you to apply justice mercifully! Some things are so basic to us and only by deliberate avoidance do we move from the truly good things intended for us. Brothers and sisters, that is for you and me. We are not speaking of heavy theology and extended periods of dialogue. Yes, and who needs a whole series of retreats and seminars to tell us what we already know? While quality events such as these are helpful for some people, who does not already perceive God in his/her life? Indeed, our needs may be decidedly more social than theological.

Spiritual direction has become very important in the last two generations. It has cut across all denominational boundaries and most all of us are in favor of it. So much spiritual growth appears to have come from it. But, let's ask some questions. Have some become virtually dependent on it? Do some have to consult their director before action or no action all the time? Can it become so all encompassing we must consult our director, even to tell us simple things we innately know? These questions are not in any sense to be taken as cynical. They are to elevate the most priceless connection of all: our personal relationship with Jesus Christ, Savior and Lord.

35

Gratefully, our lives and deaths must be seen in opportunities. We admit there are just so many opportunities and we are correct, at least, as far as we can determine. We have an ongoing impediment of being finite! Yet, this truly is a good and wholesome way of coping with life and death. As affluent Americans, many of us know what it is to have ample financial resources. Many retirees have time and reasonably good health. Indeed, some of them work wonders and do much-needed ministry. We are indebted to them over and over. When we are able to add some goodness to another's life, every day can become a beautiful thing to behold.

It is amazing — yes, even fascinating — to observe our lives and others, as they relate to opportunities. Some of us are truly grateful and can hardly wait to get up every morning to see what the day brings. Woven into all of that, of course, is God's justice. We are called to perceive and utilize each and every opportunity. Pastors are privileged in the highest and best sense. For example, people trust us with their weddings and funerals. Usually, we are paid a sum of money. Not everyone thinks we should take it but many of us do because we can take whatever amount it is and give it away, hopefully in cash and anonymously. These can be unique and heaven-sent events!

As we minister to people in the parishes, occasionally we come across those who are near death's door and claim they have missed too many opportunities. Their entire stream of thought and conversation is one of allowing so much of life to escape unfulfilled. It can be a dreary time of sadness and heartbreak. Sensitive pastors and laity struggle with what to say to them. After all, if they are eighty years of age, what do we say to them? Do we suggest they pray for more time? Do they pray God's justice will be greatly tempered by his mercy? Do we pressure them to confess their sins and start anew? The list of questions can go on and on. Most of all, we must impress upon them that God still loves them.

One of the paramount lessons we can teach our children and grandchildren is to spot opportunities that will not only benefit them, but others as well. To put it in media is one thing but to give firsthand illustrations is quite another. Of course, it is not an either/or situation; it is a both/and full opportunity. We can be highly

selective. That might play well at first. Then, we can move to showing them to live in our world is to have continual chances for doing
good to others and for ourselves. Granted, the wrong mindset can
grab for doing evil and implementing bad things. However, why
even introduce them to such negativity? As they become older, they
will rather quickly see the downside to opportunities.

Magnetically, we know there is a solution in our yearning. Justice is always and forever in God's hands. Our limitations will not
allow us to see all of this to its end. Only God will be presiding
now and forevermore. But there is a certain magnetism, isn't there?
The Holy Spirit draws us to what is right and profitable. We do so
knowing love is patient and kind; furthermore, it is not jealous or
boastful. Those who have grown up in religious families know these
truisms better than most. Give thanks for family trees that culti-
vated religious principles now and set in motion for the future.

We love our blessed Lord's kingdom and we are drawn to it. In
worship, study, and prayer we sense these are ways not only to
come to his kingdom but to stay in it all our days. It is a magnificent scene that never ever loses its magnetism. The lure of its lovely
gardens and luscious fruit remains intact. Only the subtle temptations of the devil and sometimes horrific onslaughts he sends cloud
our days and give nearly overwhelming darkness to our nights.
The best of all is that the completion of our journey will find us
safe and sound in his kingdom, never to be threatened again. Why
be downcast, except temporarily? The king of the universe is on
his throne and no one — not even all the devils in hell — can
change that.

Lent places before us more than a time of preparation to celebrate the resurrection of our Christ and God. It speaks to us about
justice the year around and how seasons come and go but his justice abides forever. While it is a portion of the church year, it in-
fluences everything else we do because the crucifixion/resurrec-
tion event is the primary basis upon which our holy faith is built.
The solution to our yearning is there in blazing and blissful truth
that seeks to draw others to its forever-living message. Yes, we are
to do more than politely go through the motions of Lent and its

disciplines! Can worldly and secular powers offer us anything approximating this? Absolutely not.

Count your blessings and name them one by one. Well, that is simple and yet profound at the same time. While it would take a long time to count all of them, the gospel communicates one blessing we must not forget. God does not leave us like beggars with no spiritual food or drink. It is there for the taking and to top it off we are drawn to it. Regardless of what befalls us, God's justice reigns and rules. Why refuse the magnetic impulses that come to us? We are his sheep and lambs. The Shepherd invites us to stay close by. Near him we will not spiritually want for anything. Our restless hearts find his abode to be exactly what we need. Indeed, so much for so little because, after all, it is all a gift from whom all blessings come.

Our Lord tells us that unless we repent we will perish. He also wants us to know, after a time, we are to bear fruit or cease to exist. Prominently brought into play is a troublesome, but always present, meaning of justice. We have our doubts about people and situations. Did they get what they deserve? Go back as far as you like in our Judeo-Christian tradition and the always challenging phenomenon is with humankind. Our text succinctly moves to the forefront the issue for all who call themselves followers of the Christ. In a tidy scriptural passage we have problems proposed and solutions given. We are not without light!

Especially as we move along in years, we are drawn to what the Lord expects of us. In fact, it may take the form of his expectations years ago. Have we done our repenting and made use of our opportunities? Is there time for healing and reconciliation not only with God but our brothers and sisters, both Christian and non-Christian? Yes, there is just so much time in this life. We must treat every day as a gift from God. Each second that ticks away belongs to us and it does not return. We do not strive for perfection as much as holiness of heart which insists we make use of every moment in serving Christ and his church in the broadest sense. So, if you haven't done so, repent. Then, make sure you bear fruit the remainder of your life.

The Two Prodigals

The relationship between and among siblings is a study both intriguing and challenging. Many of us know the truth here first-hand from the experience of growing up in families. Even if one happens to be an only child, we are brought in touch with brothers and sisters in other families.

A great deal is made of the birth order in a family. For example, the oldest son has traditionally been known as the child who is to make his mark in the world and, in some cases, look after parents and those siblings who are younger. Frequently, the youngest child is seen as "the baby," who gets special privileges.

Oh, yes, we know the dynamics, don't we? Joys and sorrows abound. Successes and failures come and go. Tragedy and triumph are there to see. Who is the most successful? Who does mother/father love the best? Don't tarnish the family name! Close ranks for the sake of family unity.

When we read the stories of the so-called great of this world, often some of the most captivating accounts involve siblings. On the current scene the Bush and Kennedy families receive lots of attention. In a sense we only need to look inside our own to note our curiosity.

The younger son went out and brazenly sowed his wild oats. Was he bored or just wanted to stretch his wings? Perhaps, neither one nor the other is the right answer but the two do point to causes that get people in trouble — regardless of age or station in life. Haven't we all been there and done that? We just get tired of the "same old same old" and decide that there has to be a better way to live in this world of ours. Boredom over an extended period of time can be almost maddening for enterprising people. Then, doesn't everyone have the right to seek growth situations? We are here to stretch and not atrophy.

How long did it take him to squander his inheritance in sordid living — days, weeks, months, or years? Apparently, no answer is to be found in the holy scriptures. Frankly, it sounds like it might have taken quite a while. There are similar situations all around us. Who among us cannot cite the young man or woman who headed out with Dad's (or Mom's) money in hand to some exciting place to have a really good time? Perhaps, like the younger son, the venture ends up being experiences of sex, booze, drugs, and the like. Then, it comes time — broken and downtrodden — for him/her to come home. The most terribly sad tales are of those who never came home and died in squalor.

The whole idea of sowing wild oats has been deeply ingrained in our culture for generations. It was thought necessary and even a rite of passage, especially for youthful males. For some years, we have witnessed the acceptance of young women also entering into this experience. While our reaction may be negative to both, something far more sinister has come into the picture of today's living. Sowing wild oats may very well continue for a lifetime! Morally, there is no settling in and becoming a decent contributing member of society. Some seem to spend all their days moving from one relationship to another and rationalize it by noting its charm and practicality. Yes, it is past time for us to cry out to God for help!

To die of hunger is a tragedy far beyond what most of us can understand. The media sometimes gives us graphic pictures and more details than suits our temperaments. The younger son is dying of hunger and lives on a level much lower than his father's hired hands. We observe the interplay of both material and spiritual hunger. To the benefit of many, we have learned the two are really closely related. Our blessed Lord tells us to be spiritually right with him is to feed the hungry and he doesn't say just to pass out attractive Bibles! The message is clear and is not always easy for some of us to accept the clarity of it immediately. We can be so engrossed in writing sermons or some other worthy venture, the truth escapes us!

The elder son was consistent, hard working, and faithful. He must have been the epitome of what the firstborn son should do and be. We can look upon him and note that he is likely holding up the good name of the family. He is probably picking up after the mistakes of an aged father and had formerly worked around the younger fellow, who likely had never earned his weight. He was solid as a rock and gave the whole family a sense of stability and security, especially as the father grew older. We don't ask our sons and daughters to emulate the younger son. We say become like the elder son.

So, what is our experience along this line? Perhaps, one of us is the oldest in the family and senses the pressures to be close to perfect for the sake of the family name and ours. It is not an easy role, at least for those known to me. Expectations are high and maybe even impossible in a real world. Those who are conscientious deserve our respect and maybe even our admiration. Some family units owe nearly their entire success to such people. This may be less true today than in yesteryear, but it is still true to some extent. We have known those who earned our sympathy. They tried their best to measure up but just could not do it. Their faltering was more noticeable because, after all, they were supposed to succeed for themselves and others.

When the young wastrel returned, it was reported to the older son. How appropriate! He was out working in the field, just as he had been all his adult years. You could set your clock by a fellow like that and not be disappointed. No doubt the neighbors praised his work ethic and loyalty to his father. We all want children like that, sons or daughters. Yes, it is a matter of pride but also the sense of seeing fulfillment for good in the family. We thank God for them and sing their praises, usually to others. Maybe in this case there just weren't enough open signs of approval. In fact, it sounds like he was being taken for granted. He didn't mind being faithful but why give recognition to his brother, who turned out to be a first-class bum?

Initially, as we read the story, aren't we on the side of the elder son? Early on, it seems mostly an open and shut case of who is right and who is wrong. One fellow is head and shoulders above the other. There is no contest and little or no debate. One keeps the home fires burning and the other shows us his nature is that of a parasite. One knows that when the going gets tough, the tough get going. The other is so morally soft he winds up eating with pigs. There is so much to be said positively about the elder one. In the other case, it is difficult to find something remotely resembling anything positive! Our hats go off to the superior son.

The younger son came into an awareness and did the right thing. He admitted to himself the party was over. It is possible he was so emaciated he was hard to recognize. Maybe that's when he truly came to himself and did so remembering with great fondness and exhilarating appreciation his former life. It had been quite a time of planting pernicious seed and now the harvest was being grievously gathered. He had learned internally and externally that whatever we do in life has a result to it. Yes, he was reaping what he had sown. There was nothing pretty about the picture but there was hope. Why? Because he knew what fatherly goodness was and prepared to go back to it.

In a way, his story is one of all of us. We may not have been promiscuous, sexually or otherwise, but we were far from knowing Jesus as Savior and Lord. There was a void of major proportions. Christ may not have been berated or declared inconsequential, but he may very well have been totally ignored. Yes, and can't we do this in the most marvelously, socially approved ways? We may be eating high-priced steak and drinking fine wine, but somehow cannot get through our heads we need to come home to the Father! It seems to me that Christ is especially concerned about such types because they remain blind and too proud to cry out to the Father.

As he repented and declared that he was no longer worthy to be a son, the angels and all the heavenly hosts must have sung songs of jubilation. Ah, what a time to celebrate a lost son being found! The father is overjoyed and tears must have been streaming down those once sorrowful cheeks. Nothing would be too good for this young prodigal who had been to the far country and now had returned. He was beaten up badly and probably smelled like the pigs that may have been the closest thing to friends he had. A gala

42

event would mark the return of him who had thrown away not only his material resources but himself as well.

So, we have placed before us the story, most likely ours as well, of one who trampled on his inheritance and the good will of his father. We can relate to that! Despite our civilized and sometimes sophisticated ways, you and I are prodigals. The only difference among us is that some have returned home and others have not. It is much like saying all are sinners, some are saved by the grace of God and others are not. To come to oneself in the highest and best sense is a remarkable gift which God enables to happen. It takes humility, sincerity, and honesty to admit our dependent place before God, doesn't it? The prodigal trudges from a foul-smelling pigpen to his father's front yard with flowers blooming, birds singing, and the aroma of forgiveness in the air.

The elder son belittled his brother and did the wrong thing. What's all this music and dancing about? Maybe my father has finally noticed what a good boy I am! Maybe my pet sheep has brought the highest price ever at the livestock market! Maybe my name will appear at last on our biggest grain barn! Maybe my father is presenting me with all that is his and no one else will even be considered! Well, that isn't very complimentary, is it? Is it realistic? Sorry to say, most likely it is because we can perceive his mindset, cold heart, and unforgiving spirit. He had been found out. He was simply being himself.

Obviously, he is not a prodigal and yet he is far from the virtues necessary to forgive his once-decadent brother. But, wait a minute. Wouldn't you be angry, too? Dumb-dumb little brother threw away what his family had accumulated for him. He displayed disdain for the very people, especially his father, who had loved him and supported him. What does anyone owe this degenerate? Oh, yes, unquestionably yes, there is a legitimate point provided here. It would take many adjectives with strong negative tones to describe this guy. When we apply a common standard of fair play, this hedonistic son is a real loser. Who is more justified than the elder in taking offense at the stupidities of a wayward brother?

With the attitude and tone of "Mr. Perfect," the father's heart must be breaking. Yet, he manages to reiterate that his son, who was dead has now come to life. He also affirms the elder son and wants him to know he remains a very important son, who shares in all the father has. The father, even in the face of impudence and unbelievable jealousy, does not reprimand him or even indicate his totally selfish behavior. Are we listening? There really are two prodigals and in our time we are called to live the Christian life in full realization that that's the way things are. Our Heavenly Father pleads with us to learn, and learn well, lessons presented.

Much of the commentary over the generations and even centuries tend to come down on the side of one prodigal son who lived despicably and then revived triumphantly. The elder brother is either something of a nonfactor or a misunderstood fellow caught in unpopular circumstances. Truly, he is also a prodigal and we hope and pray the parable is not the complete story. A more inspiring conclusion would discover he repented of his arrogance and lack of mercy. Furthermore, we long to hear him tell his father that he is grateful for all that has been given him. It would be an inspirational appendage and appear to fulfill a gospel narrative we have known from our earliest days in Sunday school or other forms of Christian education. But we are not authorized to write holy writ!

Two sons and their father are forever with us in seriously living out the faith. Despite the majority viewpoint, both are prodigals. One has returned home and the other is physically home, but not spiritually home. What a story! These fellows have all kinds, sizes, and shapes of problems. One has the humility and sincerity to seek honest solutions. The other wonders why his younger brother can do what he did and get by with it. The difference, of course, is the grace of God. One accepts it and the other doesn't. There is so much of you and me in these fellows. Perhaps we understand ourselves to be above them. Well, look again!

Truly, dear friends, the message is quite clear. Both are in need of the salvation of our Savior and Lord, Jesus Christ. Now, let's include ourselves and the rest of humankind. To be prodigal sons and daughters is no disgrace. To continue to be — even when the Holy Spirit pleads with us — is the major problem of every precious human being. Lent is an exceptional time to fall on our knees and unhurriedly seek the riches of the Christian message, delivered long ago. Yes, softly and tenderly Jesus is calling us home. Yes, oh, gentle Savior, pass me not and hear my humble cry. Yes, he touched me and made me whole. Our days are numbered but praises be to the living God there is today and maybe tomorrow.

Holy Extravagance

In our spiritual voyages, surprises — sometimes outlandishly — come to us. We scratch our heads and wonder if what we are experiencing is fact or fiction. It may or may not be a time of inspiration. However, it may be one of instruction, as we view it in retrospect. You and I are to remember that every occurrence may very well be a teaching event.

Mary's act near the time of Jesus' crucifixion is a scene mostly outside of our expectations and predictions. It catches us off guard and the same may have been true for those actually there long ago. Perhaps she caught them at an off moment and they quietly gasped in near horror.

Are we surprised by religious experiences today? In truth there are so many expressions it would take something quite bizarre to make us stand up and actually notice. Of course, when we leave that broadening field of what we define as "Christian," there is a far greater chance of being astonished. Yes, and that may not be all bad!

The Lenten season is well on its way to being over and we are summoned to take a close look at its happenings, some were bizarre and yet were expressing strong love and commitment. Who would not want to have been there? Seeing no hands go up, we are urged to continue.

We are taught that the presence of Jesus is what really counts. When we get up every morning, that should be our theme song. He walks with us and talks with us in our joys and sorrows all day long. There is a blessed fragrance that fills the air. We don't know if it is costly or not and it doesn't seem to be important one way or the other. As we move about, it moves with us. Who can put a price tag on this? In dollar bills, we know no one can. In the context of his immense suffering for us, you and I kneel before his sacrifice. Then, we praise God the Father for the love shown us in his Son, Jesus Christ, forever and ever.

When we go to bed at night, we say, "Thank you" several times. We do that more for ourselves than for him. To be sure, he desires our full compliance. On our pillows and in our beds there is this fragrance. After a time we are not shocked. We come to expect it. If we are truly in tune with the Holy Spirit, every night is memorable because we ask him to take care of us and he does. Perhaps you have found that special prayers — yes, even holy communion — are a preliminary to a night of solid sleep and relaxation. We are not only loved, we are protected by one who knows us best! Dear ones that is comforting!

The house was filled with his fragrance. Are our homes or residences also filled with this blessed aroma? Fathers and mothers, if that is not the case, then why not? Yes, there is the "hurry" button that continually gets pressed. Good parents have learned they have to fight for quality time together. They are willing to do so because they just love the aroma of Christ in them and about them! Take your own survey among those professing Jesus Christ as Savior and Lord. They desire more than anything else the precious and priceless perfume of him who died and arose again. The most brilliant of Frenchmen can neither produce it nor provide it. What a treasure Mary illustrates for us!

We reside in a world that is smelly in ways frequently offensive and, in fact, can cause us to vomit. It's the moral and ethical dimension, isn't it? Sordid politics, masking as do-good philosophy, is one we discover that especially frustrates and angers us. The plus sign is that we are able to recognize and name it for what it is. We are not helpless because the presence of Christ is about to come into the most rotten situations imaginable. How do we know? Simply, it has done it before. You and I know all things are possible with God. We are to trust and obey, for there is no other way to begin to right people and situations that are very wrong. Our confidence is nothing other than the good news being repeated and elevated.

We are taught that exuberance has a place in vital religious experience. Mary is a woman who is not going to be denied. She wasn't there to be passively watching for ways not to cause anyone a problem. Shocking others at a dinner party probably didn't interest her. If they were accepting or scandalized, all well and good. She wanted to make a point and she did. Like us, in special situations, she probably didn't have a clue as to the full impact of her actions. If poor Judas Iscariot didn't like it, maybe he should go elsewhere and lump it! The Christian faith has always needed people like her and we are better because of them. Not to feel comfortable may very well be what you and I need.

Tried and true religious behavior has a way of locking certain patterns in place. We can eventually go through the motions and little else. We can be frozen in place and become even immobilized to the point of reflecting "goodness gone to seed." Diminishing returns are all about us and, sadly, you and I may even become satisfied with our spiritual lives. Our need is for Mary or someone like her to come on the scene and into our nonproductive refrigerators to thaw us out! Then we have the possibility of spiritual good coming to us. Our pressing need for the fragrance only the Holy Spirit can provide can be met. It may be best not to ask questions but only savor the moment.

The very idea of Mary anointing Jesus' feet and wiping them with her hair was probably repugnant to others besides Judas Iscariot. There is, however, no record of their objections. To my knowledge, there is no precedent for it. She provided a shocker. Those outside of the faith today may question her sanity or perhaps pass it off as an excessively emotional woman who needed to do some odd deed to work off her frustration. It needs to be said that radically following Christ can lead any one of us into conduct the world reports as off-the-wall. Those Christians just didn't make much sense to a pagan, ancient culture. Unconditional surrender to Christ in our day and time doesn't make much sense in ours, either.

Don't you just love Mary's gall? And to think we are reading, studying, and preaching about it today. Who would have thought the fathers of the church would include the story in holy scripture? Ah, but wait a minute, we have the answer to that one. The Holy Spirit ordained it and it was and is so! The Bible does not provide us with a take it or leave it posture. To be in the scriptures is to have credibility. We attempt to talk our way out of it and away from it at our own peril. Our correct response is appreciation, gratitude, and teachability. Our Lord says to come and learn from him because he is the way, the truth, and the life.

We are taught that those who pose for good are dangerous. Poor Judas Iscariot, but let's take him for what he is. Was he really thinking about people in poverty? That has already been answered for us. All of this perfume that could bring in tons of money and you waste it on Jesus' feet! Maybe if we didn't already know Jesus, we would have bought into the treasurer's comment. After all, he was an apostle and there were only twelve of them. Yes, he was posing for good and, if you didn't know him, he made quite a good impression. We know some people like that, don't we? Sometimes their posturing is a sight to behold!

You and I can be gullible. We focus our attention on people resembling the fellow in question. Apparently, he kept the common purse and used to steal from it. Talk about corruption in high places! But, there is a lesson here and God's people are urged to learn it as early as possible. Beware of those who tout their goodness. Every church and church organization, which have been in operation for any length of time, knows the embarrassment and even disillusionment going with this foul smell. The media frenzy eats up pages of print and expensive time on both radio and television.

Despite those who parade a philosophy of the natural goodness of humankind, original sin seems to be about as lethal as it ever was. Those well-meaning souls who think human nature is continuing to get better had best look again. This is not a pessimistic view. It is realistic and finds its source in holy scripture. Admittedly, we have come a long way in racial and gender equality. Yet, even then, we forget or refuse to admit that our primary goal is to accept the fact that everyone is equally important before God and we are to treat one another with that in mind. It is not possible for human ingenuity to provide full equality for every man and woman, largely because the definition of "equality" is different for different people.

In a way, Judas Iscariot is unwittingly part of a positive family gathering, immersed in spiritual fragrance. Had we asked him, he certainly would never have allowed such holy extravagance! Maybe we are too harsh and should listen one more time to some scholars who insist he was predestined to do what he did. That is a bit of a stretch for some of us and, thank God, the truth is in his hands and beyond our puny comprehensions. The episode can grow complicated and a project for academics. In the meantime, you and I are inspired to live the Christian life. We know it is wrong to pose for good and our depths sense the hypocrisy gravitating to the forefront.

We are taught the cries of the poor must be heard, but Jesus comes first. Jesus orders Mary to be left alone. Furthermore, he says the costly perfume is to be used for the day of his burial. His strange statement indicates the poor will always be around but he won't. Our initial response may be along the lines of his primacy in our ministries and the fundamental reason we do them. Briefly, we feed and aid the poor because Jesus the Christ challenges us to do so. Our core for doing meaningful ministry is found in him and none other. Another way of looking at it is to show that there is only a short time left on earth for him and it is imperative he be placed first.

The centrality of Christ in the life of the church emerges originally because of his physical presence among us. Had our Lord just sent his ideas by way of Peter, James, John, and Paul, where would the Jesus movement be today? Likely, a well-developed theology and/or philosophy in books on the shelves of libraries would be its lot. It took flesh and blood! Indeed, it took his body and blood in the form of a sacrament to provide for a holy extravagance imparted to his friends. Had there been no physical Jesus literally walking and talking among us, the power of our religion would be so diminished that we could hardly visualize its relevance. He was God in the flesh.

51

The world needed a man who could see, hear, feel, taste, and smell. There were thousands of gods in the ancient culture in which our Lord entered. Not one of them was human in the real sense. Oh, there were the Caesars but so what? Ruthlessness characterized most of them. There was very little compassion and they were not going to die for anyone. That is, they were not going to die for anyone if they could keep from it. The Father, it seems, asked, "So you want to see God?" Then, he added, "Well, don't go away, because my only Son is being sent to you. Yes, dear people, he will live with you and die for you, Jesus is the supreme sacrifice. Beyond him there is none other. So, come now, and enjoy the riches of the faith."

Do we need to know more? No, only that overarching burst of truth coming straight from the Father. Provision is made for us in all ways in a world known for its countless saviors. The Father announces Jesus is his Son and he is pleased with him. We are to receive him as Savior and Lord. In all ways, you and I are given the mandatory ingredients for being born again and inheriting eternal life. Why shouldn't Mary anoint his feet? We can take care of the poor, too! Oh, such completeness is ours as a gift from the living God. Indeed, what holy extravagance! The good news keeps coming to us in a myriad of ways. Celebrate today, tomorrow, and the next day. Our Lord will celebrate with us.

You and I, like others across the centuries, were invited to a dinner. The principal characters are Mary, Martha, Lazarus, and Judas Iscariot. It was a memorable gathering, as Mary anointed her Lord's feet with expensive perfume. The one who betrayed Jesus made quite an issue out of her act. He thought the money the perfume cost should have been used for the poor. The sad thing is, he was a thief and his do-gooder approach carried no weight. The Master affirmed Mary's generous act and indicated that the poor are always with us, yet he will not be with them much longer.

We learn there is a holy extravagance about the event. It is discovered in the presence of Christ bringing with it a singular fragrance the world can neither produce nor give away. The spirituality of our Master makes for victory in all circumstances, mainly because we are teachable. Mary was not a loose cannon looking for notoriety and an elevated place in Christ's kingdom. Her generous deed was one for the benefit of all concerned there and then, plus all those who followed and professed the Christ. Her selflessness and lack of fear continue to shine for all to view. How preciously beautiful all of it is! If the Father really calls us to step out of the humdrum of social relationships and do something extraordinary, may the Father, during this Lenten season, grant you the strength to do it.

History Hangs In The Balance

One would be hard pressed to find a historical event with so many ramifications equal to these words from Saint Luke's Gospel. In fact, for the devout Christian there is no other! It is a moment when the universe seems to come to a standstill and the angels watch in troubled awe.

You and I observe from afar, indeed, a great distance. Unless we figuratively or literally read the passage on our knees, we are not apt to catch this sublime, serious moment. Yes, and our appreciation may very well remain at surface level, more or less. It is not a moment of timidity but one of pure gratitude.

Historians and theologians record these events today. It is nearly impossible to do so without commentary that shows biases and that is not all bad! Our faith is based upon a few historical happenings that bring earth and heaven together. Explanations simply beg to be given.

While the gospels do not give identical accounts, we cannot miss the similarities. Our Lukan passage is straightforward and would appear not to sugarcoat anything. For that alone, our thanksgivings should be heard throughout the universe.

His innocence is emphasized but guilt prevails. Pilate kept saying over and over that there was not enough evidence to crucify him. The Roman prefect of Judea was the second-longest holder of the office, apparently for ten years or so. In a time of virtually omnipresent intrigue, he was a survivor. It was manifest that he wanted to do the right thing. There just was not enough evidence to convict Jesus for major crimes and have him put to death. Would

55

or could Jesus be considered innocent until proven guilty? The mob would see to it that that would not happen. Innocence of serious charges was not relevant!

Perhaps some of us perceive a goodness and fairness in Pilate that is not allowed to carry the day. It certainly seems he is guided by a sense of justice and fairness. We are close to admiration and begin to wonder if he is an innocent party himself, caught in a web of power politics with a strong, religious overtone. Well, he does disappoint us and yields to the political realities at hand. A man in his position cannot allow substantial unrest in the area assigned to him by Caesar. When it comes to preserving number one and a place of power, we know who and what almost always wins.

The power structure among the Jews insists Jesus is guilty. It seeks no other verdict. It is time to be rid of this pesky fellow who stirs up the people and irritates the ruling Romans. This is not to maintain Jews were generally guilty then ... or now. We must be careful — even astute — in handling such a delicate matter. To do otherwise is not only to ask for criticism but to open ourselves to outright dishonesty and even flagrant anti-semitism. If we have stretched our ecumenical and interreligious wings, we know that Jewish people cannot only be friendly they can be friends and even comrades. That is cause for "hallelujahs"!

The hallmark of the situation shows the forces of sinful men colliding with one another and the mysteries of God working themselves out. Do the people responsible for our Lord's crucifixion desire to fight it out with God? Do they believe the will of God does not eventually prevail? Are they deliberately selecting and insisting upon an avenue of action opposed to their Creator? Maybe our answers to such inquiries are summed up in "of course not." The ferocious frenzy to declare him guilty, so crucifixion can take place, may be experienced by you and me as totally irrational and motivated solely by prejudice. But have we forgotten what mobs can do to the innocent? If we have, our memories should be jogged by the lynchings of thousands recorded in our nation.

His followers and friends objected but they are to be pitied. We know his disciples, as well as others, were not at all in agreement with this maddening spectacle. While mostly unrecorded, those who could and did follow him must have said their piece. Since they, at that time, appeared to come mostly from those without significant place and power, what chance did they have in turning back the juggernaut? Let's be honest. The sobering answer is "very little — if any." Their objections fell on the deaf ears of those who controlled the situation. Who can blame them for their lack of bravery and courage? Are you and I ready to cast stones?

Isn't it amazing the success stories, especially all the healings recorded in Saint Luke's Gospel, have so quickly and unceremoniously gone down the tubes? The meteoric character of his career was there for many to witness. What went wrong? For 2,000 years we have probed this matter. We seem to keep trying to make the story turn out differently. Let's be honest and admit that we are stumped and so much doesn't make sense in the way we want! It isn't enough that our salvation is the outcome. We are tempted to keep on telling the story in a way which communicates that we think it should have happened some other way. In fact, just maybe we could have improved it.

Pity enters at the juncture of visualizing the faithful making little or no difference in the drama unfolding. Why are they so helpless? We suspect there is much cowardice at work. If there is, we would rather not observe it. After all, weren't the earliest of disciples the best and most determined to follow him of all? Shame on you people who objected so meekly and inconsequentially! He told you to be prepared to lay down your lives for your friends and he was the best friend you ever had. Our pity can lead almost instantaneously to a top-heavy judgmental attitude. In short, we accuse people of doing the very things we do.

For some, his unwillingness to save himself must have really irked them. Common sense said there was no good reason for this tragic event to occur. If you are who you say you are, why hesitate in throwing the cross in their faces and walk away victoriously? That's all it would take and the Romans would back down to keep the peace. The Jews, who opposed him, would be discredited and the Master could finish years of essential ministry. As usual with them, plus you and me, salvation history is being made and we refuse to recognize it. How true of our spiritual pilgrimages today!

The blessed Lord works in us and through us but we find fault with what is transpiring. Original sins just never seem to go away.

His detractors and enemies jeered but he called for forgiveness. Not only did they shout "crucify him," they sought to hurt and embarrass him at every opportunity. Just to take him out and kill him was not nearly enough. The Master had to undergo punishment after punishment. Most of us do not have the imaginations to get close to the reality of all of this. It was truly hell on earth for a man — believe it or not — who pleaded for them to be forgiven. Perhaps the closest we get to the sordid scene is the experience of some prisoners of war. Your captors want you to suffer in great pain before they kill you. The longer death can be put off, the better!

Sprinkled throughout church history are saints who enacted the Lord's call to forgive enemies. Those who hurt them the most were those they begged God to forgive. Can we speak a word about ourselves here? If the answer is in the affirmative, are we prepared to be guided by pristine honesty? We are mostly fair-weather Christians, aren't we? We relish being known for our regular worship attendance and tithing. Those disciplines alone put us above the average and we are self-satisfied. If everyone just did as much as we do, what a wonderful world it would be and how strong the churches would become! We may be tempted to think enough of that and walk on with heads held high, proclaiming our exemplary conduct.

Sometimes we hear serious-minded people saying they don't like God. Well, how can you like an eternal being who tells you to forgive those who harm, humiliate, and hate you in ways totally nonsensical? So, now we come into the area of the nature of God. If Jesus Christ is God in the flesh, then what he says must not only be true, but followed. That helps, doesn't it? We may not want to accept it. We may even find it repugnant. Nevertheless, to be true to our Savior and Lord, we have received our orders. Here we come to terms with what human nature prods us to do and what our Master summons us to do. It is an ongoing tension and with merely human feelings, a terrifying truth.

How can people want to destroy someone as well-meaning and pure as the Man of Galilee? What good or contribution is there in him being crucified? Here we enter the "unreasonable reasonableness" dimension of our salvation. An enigma is presented. A contradiction seemingly irreconcilable makes its way into our minds. Wouldn't it be better just to ignore or evade the guy? We are now getting someplace. Christ was so strong in person and message that people who were around him were pushed to be for or against him. His opposition had mounted. They absolutely refused to change, plus there were those who always wanted to please the power brokers. It is the same story told today across our planet.

His death brought supernatural happenings but the spectacle prevailed. The Lord's demise has brought us to the door of discovery. The criminal has been promised paradise and darkness has covered the land for three awful hours. Then, Jesus cries out to his Father, commending his Spirit to God. They were left with very mixed feelings and thoughts. Whom do we mean by "they"? The answers are many and it is not unlikely there was even something close to unanimity among his own followers. To be sure, the Lord's hardcore enemies must have been ecstatic and yet with the darkness, in particular, must have sensed a fear they had not experienced before. At the other extreme those who loved him deeply must have felt the best part of their lives was over.

The centurion perhaps said the only words that made sense. He praised God and called Jesus innocent or — better still — righteous. There was the crystal-clear recognition that this man, so maligned, was someone very special and God was much in the brutal and inhumane scene. It is as though the Roman officer perceived he had just witnessed an event never to be forgotten with God entering history in a supernatural way. We may take it to mean God has allowed the death of a righteous man for a purpose so meaningful and unforgettable that we have only seen the beginning of its import for generations to come. The everlasting and living God gives his gift.

To say the least, it was a spectacle at the moment no one could understand. However, there must be a sense — even with the prevailing spectacle — there was more of something to come. Did

59

anyone know what that something was? Who can know for sure but the answer appears almost 100 percent to be completely in the negative. Have we been there before in a much smaller and insignificant way? Perhaps it was during the time of a major tragedy or triumph. We knew, didn't we, that we had not heard the last of it? What we did not know was what was coming, but to be sure, something more was on the horizon. What did the Lord have in store for us? Time would tell.

Yes, as they walked home beating their breasts, and the Master's followers watched at a distance, a new day was at hand. Oh, it was not yet consummated but just wait and see! We believe Luke narrates the story well and reliably. Those present did not know whether or not the worst had come and gone. There were those who remembered. He said that death and resurrection were a part of the fabric of his mission. It would be the culmination of his ministry and all of humankind would be impacted. So much now was hanging in the balance. It was the "not yet" time in salvation history. We were not there but our blessed Lord through his Holy Spirit takes us there, and we are greatly humbled but inspired beyond words to exclaim the gift at hand.

With brilliant directors and actors, Hollywood could hardly produce the colossal event presented to us. It defies human ingenuity and creativity. We are witnesses, as Christians and non-Christians alike, to the unfolding drama prepared by the Father for his Son from the beginning. Man is in a fallen state and must be rescued. It is so bad only the Son by sacrificing himself can bring about a right relationship with the Father. Everyone and everything becomes a part of the supreme revelation to precious people, who are otherwise lost in their sins. It is a no-holds-barred moment in history and failure means eternal gloom and doom.

There is something about such a defining instant — brief in anyone's measurement — that penetrates our eternal souls. It is so personal we gasp for breath and hope in painful pangs, bordering on panic. The message is to you and me, isn't it? There is no need to look around and see to whom it applies. Brothers and sisters, we are the ones crying out for a salvation that conquers death, even the worst kind. He had to die for you and me to live. He had to suffer in unconscionable agony for you and me. The ultimate price had been paid and the way was cleared for a victorious resurrection assuring others, including you and me, that there was hope only Jesus Christ could give.

A Frightening Friday

So much happening in so little time! We are left gasping for breath. We stagger under the weight of the mighty arm of historical occurrence. You and I praise God because we know the rest of the story. Those present did not know how things would turn out. They must have been like awestruck children nearing exasperation.

Those of us who have read and perhaps studied the great writers amazingly discover that Saint John tops them all. Shakespeare was truly brilliant but there is a peculiar demeanor about our lengthy passage that goes beyond his work. Dante and Milton — with others coming to mind — cause us to pause reverently in admiration but John causes us to kneel in adoration.

How can we even begin to digest all of this coming at us at one time? It is so imposing and it stretches us to limits that give us a glimpse of our immortal souls. We want to shout for everything to wait a minute or two, indeed, a year or two! Call in the wise men and women; let them brood for a time.

But now — just maybe — the Holy Spirit has provided us with enough love, faith, and hope to continue in genuine humility. Praises be to God, what an opportunity! We are privy to the unfolding and making of salvation history. It is a moment of our spirits being quickened.

Judas Iscariot betrayed his Lord. This whole business of betrayal is one which is gripping for us because we never know who will decide to sell us out. The drama of human beings relating to human beings is filled to overflowing with such nasty experiences.

Some move well into adulthood before finding out what has happened to them. Others learn in high school or even before. How about you and me? If it hasn't happened to us, it will! Yes, and not one of us has a desire to be labeled a "Judas." His name — all it conjures up — is an odious reminder of what is at hand.

How many times have we heard this man thoroughly castigated for his dastardly deed? We have probably lost track. His is an infamy that never goes away. It carries a singular stench. He betrayed our blessed Lord! He was a scoundrel and deserved the worst cell in hell. But many of us over time become more thoughtful, don't we? The scum of the earth who betrayed the greatest and most pure man to live among us is seen, at least, with some compassion and not a few questions. Was he really that bad and did he have a will of his own to prevent his name being remembered forever as the epitome of a traitor? You and I cannot condone what he did, and Christ tells us not to judge.

What are the motives behind his actions? Some say he was a Jewish patriot who wanted the hated Romans driven from the land. He was patient with Jesus for a time and began to see there was no hope for this to happen. Others maintain that he was a crook from the beginning and wanted only to handle the little band's money. He would then steal cleverly from that precious treasury to promote himself. Yes, it is even thought the devil so totally dominated his motives there was no other way for him to behave. Could he have been predestined? Haven't we seen people, who despite their apparent good intentions, never seem to come out on the right side of anything?

While you and I see ourselves, for the most part, as quite distant from his perfidy, are we really? If Christ and his church do not say what we want to hear, what is our response? Sometimes good people betray their pastors. Sometimes good pastors betray their people. To be sure, these are exceptions, but our personal stories cannot be told accurately from our internal struggles that are only known by us and God. To be more focused, we have all been tempted to betray somebody. The evil one tells us that is not the way something should be and we are led into a trap. To correct the situation, the evil spirit skillfully sells us on betraying someone we have loved and supported. So, the question becomes one of accepting or rejecting the bait made to look necessary for all concerned.

Simon Peter showed his cowardice. Peter invariably seemed to get the attention of the gospel writers. He was the dominant apostle, regardless of whether he was doing good or ill. He ran the gamut of cowardly bum to sacrificial saint. Of course, we would only see the latter after the resurrection and the day of Pentecost. He was the most unlikely of the twelve — except Judas Iscariot — to provide leadership for the ancient church. How could someone be such a bumbling idiot? His Lord had called him close different times, giving his insight into the future. It is as though he heard a different drummer. He had the close confidence of his Lord and worked overtime to negate that beloved relationship.

At this cataclysmic point in time, there just doesn't appear to be much hope for him. All he was capable of doing was slipping around on the fringes telling folks he doesn't know the Man of Galilee. After all that his Savior had seen him through, he was apparently scared out of his wits some people would connect him to the fellow about to be crucified. What a loser! It was indeed a frightening Friday and Peter was one of the biggest ducks in the puddle. He was so far removed from the imperative loyalty to lead the Jesus movement, we scratch and dig around to find something with which to defend him.

Just the simple word, "coward," causes many of us to shiver and shake. Is there ever anyone who wants to be described as one? Except in jest and playfulness, we don't like any part of that word. Oh, we might like it applied to someone else who strongly disagrees with us or does something we can't tolerate. Even then, it has a way of cluttering up our understanding of religious and moral perceptions. We would just as soon it not appear in our dictionaries and vocabularies. In a sober moment of pondering, we admit that if we took it out, we would have to find another word to define what certainly is a fact of life! Yes, history books indicate it is not an uncommon trait.

Peter's fate turned out to be infinitely better than that of Judas Iscariot. Who could tell at the time how things would turn out? It looked like a big zero was the answer. So, what is the difference?

Is it that God liked Peter a lot better than Judas? Needless to say, that is a stretch and mostly for those who want to do endless dialogue dynamics for the sake of exploring all possibilities. Perhaps the best way to understand his problem is to note that he recognized the Lord has chosen him for great things but he simply did not know what to do about it. So, he stumbled and fumbled with a generous amount of grumbles. Jesus was through with his betrayer but not his cowardly apostle.

Pilate performed his political duty. Good old Pontius Pilate! He seemed to do everything on schedule. He was a predictable politician. After apparently having such accurate and objective thoughts of God's Son, he progressively or regressively — depending on one's understanding — ended up defending what was near and dear to him: his position. To let things get out of hand was certainly to be demoted and possibly much worse. So, to survive and meet his own needs in his world, he caved in and opened the way for our Lord's hideous death. Sound familiar for politicians? You bet it does! He was right on schedule and we might even be tempted to inquire as to why he took so long.

Maybe we should inject the thought, which has much substance, that there are only two kinds of politics: good and bad. The good means most everybody wins in the highest and best sense. The bad means quite the reverse. Is Pilate reacting like most of us would react in that situation? Obviously, he was fascinated by the man whose guilt or innocence was in the balance. He had not been with Jesus in closed sessions like the apostles. He was known only at a distance. While fear and some sense of justice motivated him, he did the only thing that made sense at the time. What would you and I have done? Would we have been seriously interested in good politics? Each of us has to answer for himself or herself.

It must have been quite an ego trip to have Jesus before him and be able to convict or acquit this amazing fellow. It was an opportunity made in a pagan heaven, filled with idols and self-congratulatory weapons. He had, some would call, God in his presence, the power to destroy or release. Wow, that is something of a very special circumstance! What else could be so favorable for a man who wanted always to stay on the good side of Caesar, who many considered a deity? Perhaps there is nothing so destructive in our world as pure, unadulterated egotism: witness the likes of Adolf Hitler and many others. It was a singular and demonic instant of glory.

Pilate has not only found his way into the holy scriptures, he appears as well in both the Apostles' and Nicene Creeds. We are not apt to forget him anytime soon! His is one of the few names having been perpetuated from the times our Lord walked and talked upon this earth. He made history and his name is there for all to see. Yes, one wonders about his select place — good, bad, or otherwise. He could be called a major player or actor but it was certainly the Father's stage and the Father, contrary to what some may say, was doing all of the directing. Yes, we see only in a mirror dimly but God has the total picture, which he sees perfectly and in its totality. The majority of Christian worshipers across the globe say Pilate's name.

Mary, his mother, was given to a trusted and loving apostle. Can we even begin to imagine Mary's thoughts and feelings during these hours? She watched her son undergo a humiliating death. There he was stark naked in agony, dying like any common, ordinary thief or seditionist. Her heart must have been ripped asunder and she may have even shouted at God because it was all so unjust and unfair. Try — for a fleeting moment — to put yourself in her place. She carried him inside her body like any other mother and gave birth to him. He was a part of her body and after the birth, when she could hold him in her arms, there was that powerful sense he belonged to her. In a way she died, too. Her baby, little boy, teenager, and adult man was gone.

She is the blessed Virgin Mary to much of Christendom. What an appealing and magnificent name! She was a sublimely favored one and full of grace. The Lord was with her. She was blessed among women. The fruit (Jesus) of her womb was blessed. She is defined as the mother or bearer of God. Many ask her to pray for them at their deaths. Wow, that really was and is some extra special lady! Why is it when we speak about feminist power and priorities, she seems invariably absent? To some extent, in our day and time this is being answered and many Protestants have had their blinders lifted and she begins to move to her rightful place.

It is said on reliable authority that the apostle who received the honor or responsibility for her was John. Our Lord would look after his mother, like any good Jewish son, and so he gave her to one he must have trusted the most. It all happened just before he bowed his head and gave up his spirit. Exactly what occurs after that remains questionable, except for mention in the Acts of the Apostles. In reverential retrospect we view a son who refused to die before his mother received some security for the future. For an instant, motherhood is lifted to a new level because she bore the Son of the living God. The ages have spoken of such maternity. Catholics and Orthodox integrated her extraordinary place in the faith, centuries ago.

Hopefully, gone are the days of vitriolic arguments about her and where she belongs in our belief systems. Pope John Paul II, who spoke to many outside of the Roman Catholic church, has helped us immensely. The movement on the part of some of us in the Protestant churches has helped and is helping. Increasingly, we are experiencing evidence she is more — much more — than a woman in the right place at the right time! The healthy dialogue has caused some of us to shout praises to God, our Father, for the progress at hand. It did not come overnight but it has come to us under the guidance of the Holy Spirit. No feminine force can unite us as Christians the way Mary does. She may very well be the key to our unity.

The key players do what they do! Among them — along with Jesus — is Judas Iscariot, Simon Peter, Pontius Pilate, and the blessed Virgin Mary. How can the story of a frightening Friday be told without them? Yes, and it isn't over until it's over! The piercing of his side is not the end. The gentlemanly conduct of Joseph of Arimathea and Nicodemus, we soon learn, is not the end. We group the events together, as best we can, and wait in anticipation of the supreme victory song of salvation history. Those, centuries ago, had mixed feelings. Some thought the ignominious tailgate had come down and the Master had failed in a definitive fiasco.

The thing you and I must not do is to become lackadaisical which leads to a lackluster attitude toward Resurrection Sunday. Oh, dear Father of our Savior and Lord, please don't allow this to happen! We are reminded there is not the smallest amount of humdrum in what is taking place. We know beforehand that the gloom and doom gathers by the tons. We have to wait until a glorious victory is declared once and for all. Our brothers and sisters who were there join in an unending chorus of praise with us. Our spiritual ancestors plead with us to be vigilant and reexperience what Christ does for us. Kneel in prayerful tears of joy for atrocious events that changed our lives and deaths, now and forever. Amen.

Mary Magdalene's Day

Mary Magdalene may very well be the most enigmatic and controversial figure in the resurrection story. In a way the holy scriptures give us just enough information to excite our curiosity in regard to her personal relationship with the man she adored, Jesus of Nazareth. We still wonder what kind of person she was.

Fiction writers have had a field day, especially in recent years. Was she really married to Jesus and did they have children? Did they establish a bloodline that is with us today? Such inquiries, while they may border on blasphemy, need airing. That is not to assume our traditional revelation is in error.

Wherever we come down in our understanding of her, we are forced to admit that she was a major player in the story upon which the authenticity of our religion is based. In short, if there is no resurrected Christ, we have a philosophy and theology among others. It becomes neither unique nor especially powerful.

The debate between eastern (Orthodox) and western (Roman Catholic) Christianity shows views with some solid differences. When we enter the explanation of Protestants, we enter into an even wider and more complicated discussion. Nevertheless, there is agreement that she is someone with whom we must come to terms.

She cared deeply about Jesus. All accounts indicate there developed a strong and emotional relationship between the two. Did she love him? Of course, she did. It is that love which has provided fodder for both the believing and unbelieving grist mills. So, how is that different from countless other relationships adoring women

71

have with their "kings"? We can summon to our consciousness examples galore of some notables and others that are "down home" figures. The difference is seen in whom he claimed to be, especially in the understanding of the ancient church.

If we discovered reliable sources proving Mary Magdalene and Jesus were married and had children but otherwise his messiahship remained intact as recorded, how would you and I respond? For many this is not only an awkward inquiry but one causing us to vomit at the mere articulating of it. Jesus was celibate, perfect in all ways, and there is no reason to test — really test — it by thinking along the lines of marriage and family. The dialogue today is heated and may not go away any time soon. Opportunists are always with us and at times they can be quite convincing before we find them out. Surely open and free inquiry is imperative. In fact, this is the way Christianity has survived over the centuries.

We sure wished we knew more, don't we? It is much like parishioners who hear stories — perhaps even allegations — about their pastors and priests, except at a level of extreme importance. We know what the child abuse scandal has done to the Roman Catholic church. Whether by fact or pure supposition, the spotlight is placed on all priests. It just doesn't matter that substantiation may be no higher than three percent. She cared deeply for her Lord. On a strictly human level, those kind of relationships sooner or later cause the busybodies to come out in the open. Strong affection and great respect are not immune from Satan's clutches. The very best are tempted to become the very worst.

To notify Simon Peter first of all is to show not only that he was the leader of that faithful band of followers but her attempt to stay within the community of believers in loyalty. She could have gone to his enemies, Jewish and Roman. She seems unwilling to take credit for anything and apparently wants, first of all, to share her discovery with those within the fellowship of faith. Within itself, her approach is commendable. Her deepest thoughts must have been at the point of desiring to know if he was all right. He must have been her life in the spiritual sense. There is a message for you and me here. Our top priority is what our Savior and Lord means to us and not suspicions of so-called facts that sway our commitment.

She experienced the presence of angels. Simon Peter along with the other disciples surveyed the situation and returned to their homes. Not so with Mary! She stood outside the tomb weeping. Then, alone, she looked into the tomb and saw two angels in white. The gospel is specific in their location. One was at the head where he was lying and the other at the feet. The occasion gives rise to the skeptics who wonder why it is recorded that only she saw the angels. Was she building on her desire to have supernatural beings present? Perhaps her need to make the situation into more than it was caused angels to be seen. But don't those folks who are invariably doubting lose this one?

The conversation with the angels must have been brief; at least, that's what the record indicates. As we extend our thoughts, we discover a woman, perhaps in the grips of hysteria, who wants with all her heart to know where they have laid him. She wants to see him and probably touch him. He was her Lord. The price had been paid for our salvation and she was not about to run away. She knew firsthand what that salvation was. It was embodied in Jesus of Nazareth. Alive or dead, she wanted to know where they had laid him. Maybe it could be a sacred moment of relaying to him how much he meant to her. Surely, the crucifixion could not be the end for such a good man.

For some, the presence of angels may be very unusual. Yet, those who have studied the holy scriptures and read histories before and after Jesus' earthly existence know angels were almost commonplace. At certain points in one's life, especially birth and death, they put in an appearance. You and I may see this as mostly superstition and avoiding down-to-earth facts. But we didn't live in that world. Therefore, what is written down for future use must be taken seriously. Why quarrel with a source the universal church proclaims as integral to the revelation of our faith? Fortunately and mostly positively angels have made a serious comeback in our day and time. This may very well be a Holy Spirit reminder!

So, our dear lady, sometimes maligned and other times elevated to levels of the highest discipleship, comes to a moment of transition. Does she already know the answer is at hand? The narrative does not say so and it doesn't appear that even the angels have implied what has transpired. She must be all alone with none of the other disciples present. Others mentioned earlier have gone to their homes. What they are talking about we do not know but what we do know is Mary is alone with two angels in white. She must not have been afraid. Our suspicions are that she is not going to give up on finding the Man who must have meant more to her than life itself. She may have been the most dogged of the disciples who believed defeat was not defensible!

She recognized him by his voice. Not knowing who he was, she responded to his question of why she was weeping and for whom she was looking by supposing he was the gardener. She wanted to know where they had laid him. Then, she iterated words which bring about a multitude of questions. She says she will take him away. What right did she have to claim the body? Obviously, at that moment Mary thought he was dead. Was it because no one else wanted his broken body? Crucifixion leaves a body most ugly and, in his case, his side had been pierced. Who would want such a deformed, haggard, and discredited corpse? She did!

Ah, he says her name and she immediately knows who he is. She responds by calling him "teacher." What a meeting that must have been! Her anxious longing for her Master was gone. There he was! The man Mary expected to find in the form of a dead body was doing much more that that; he was talking to her. He had arisen from the dead, as he said he would. Other than her exclamation, we have no account of what was going through her mind. We can only guess. Would he be available for times of intimate conversation? Would everything be returned to where it was before his death? Where would he live and practice his ministry? Perhaps he would execute justice and take his killers to task by destroying them. So, there she is awaiting answers.

Does our dear Lord ever call you or me by name? We have known people who claimed as much. We are impressed by those who profess exactly that. Some build denominations and others followings which often are impressive. When we are called by our names, it makes a difference. By and large, we all like to hear them. The truth of the matter is, we not only like to hear our names but to sense a strong, even undeniable, urge. That's a normal course of life. In Mary's case it was so much more than having a relative, friend, or acquaintance blandly say the word. Our names are highly significant.

Jesus Christ reports to her that he will be ascending to his Father. But until it happens no one is to hold onto him. Just what the meaning is here has confused even the most brilliant and committed scholars. So, it is by faith and mystery we let his words rest and relax in our hearts, minds, and souls. Briefly, whatever the Lord is doing is fine with us. We know everything will come out well for those who love him and seek to follow him. There is nothing quite like putting faith in him and his ways. Mary is to tell his brothers. That within itself must have been quite innovative. Again, we encounter the relationship between the two. It means he trusts her! What higher badge or medal could she be presented? We underestimate Mary at our own peril.

She announced his resurrection. Our text says to us specifically that one of the disciples saw the empty tomb and believed. Yet, it also relates to us that they didn't understand the scripture that he must rise from the dead. So, there is no clear-cut announcement of the resurrection. It takes Mary Magdalene to do the announcing to the disciples. She reports, "I have seen the Lord." While we may get into heated conversations, it certainly sounds like she is the one who was willing to make it known. It also sounds as though she is the only one to whom he literally spoke. Indeed, it was "Mary Magdalene's Day"!

That, within itself, must have been quite a shocker. Women did not do such things then. This happening that would shake heaven and earth was an event so monumental that no one could possibly have considered that a woman would make the pronouncement. Well, there you have it again. Our Savior and Lord didn't follow protocol! She was presented an honor so profoundly marvelous that we look at her in awe. We must wonder why it was given to her. After all, there is a great deal of information saying she was a woman of questionable morals. Ah, but that was so like Jesus and his ways. Peter, James, John, and Paul would come to us as solid apostles. She would largely be in the background, smiling in glorious contentment and savoring her honor.

As is so frequently the case, the most germane inquiry is, "Have you and I seen the Lord?" Now, we have been thrilled by one of the most moving passages throughout the holy scriptures and there is this inquiry, refusing to go away. If we have not seen him, what good does it do to go on living with a miraculous affirmation and story never reenacted into our lives? It is a pressingly relevant way to get at religion, which is alive and well. Really, no other kind or variety is worth having. Not to have some conversion experience, regardless of how and when it comes about, may be the most sad void known to those who continually hear the gospel preached. Offering after offering is made through Word and sacrament. What's our response?

Don't you just love Mary Magdalene? A part of her fascination is the way she surfaces at the most crucial event in the history of Christianity. Any number of persons would likely have had it some other way. For example, surely Peter and John should have had the honors. Maybe they did more than the narrative says but we don't know that. What we assuredly know is this special woman must have been the first one to arrive at the tomb and even more significantly the one who presented the glorious information to the disciples. So, we thank her and acknowledge that God does whatever he chooses to do and with whomever he wishes. Grant that our wills be malleable and moldable for his touch.

Is it truly "Mary Magdalene's Day"? The evidence is there. The Gospels of Matthew, Mark, Luke, and, in particular, John differ. However, we learn that each of the four has a unique contribution. John's Gospel places before us a lovely story, featuring Mary Magdalene. It is immersed in emotion and we are recipients of the picture of a woman who loved and cared deeply about Jesus. He responded to her hurt and lostness. He called her by name and the heavens burst forth in songs of praises. Question what you will about her but here is a woman sold on her man. His name was Jesus and it would be known for more than 2,000 years, but so would hers.

A living relationship with the risen Jesus Christ is what counts, isn't it? Anything less will not enable us to live a victorious faith that others want. To be able to tell others we have seen the Lord and he lives in our hearts is the message the world always yearns to hear. To see his behavior in action with power and vitality makes even the hardest sinner sit up and take notice. Are we being too fundamental and, some would say, pietistic? Perhaps, but then we must discover new words to say essentially the same thing! The message of salvation delivered to humankind remains the same. We are called to be Easter or Resurrection Christians. The grave has been conquered. Heaven is a reality. What more can we ask?

Those Who Doubt

Christianity has always had its doubters. Sometimes it comes in open and public terms. Perhaps more often, despite our attempts at accurate measurements, are the doubters who speak only to intimate friends or not at all. When you and I doubt we are not alone. In the ancient world, our precious faith made little sense to most Jews or Gentiles.

Some great souls, even saints, have been born out of times of skepticism. We have always had our "doubting Thomases." Read the autobiographies and biographies of those stalwarts in church history. When the truth is fully uncovered, we discover some thoroughgoing doubters!

Well, how about you and me? In honesty and sincerity, we admit the message of Christ did not and does not always convince us. It is therapeutic and, perhaps above all, admirable to come to that place in our lives. Our pride is defeated and we admit we are not always 100 percent sure.

The Resurrection and Easter story is the one we may be tempted to water down or simply shrug our shoulders in polite disbelief. Of course, the virginal conception of our blessed Lord is another really big area of question marks! But let us not digress from our major consideration.

Thomas was very specific about his requirements for believing. Don't try to tell me you have seen the Lord, unless you have some real proof. Show me the mark of the nails, so my finger can be placed there. Yes, and my hand must touch his side. There will be no sentimental guessing and wishful thinking. There will be no misleading attempts to prove a point and pass it along to the world at large. The Master was much loved by all of us but we cannot claim too much for him and be dishonest with others, including those who need his message so desperately. Yes, it is hard to argue with our friend!

It is recorded that Jesus had already been among a select group of disciples. He showed them his hands and side. He spoke to them and breathed upon them the gift of the Holy Spirit. The forgiving and retention of sins is even placed upon them. What more could anyone possibly ask? Surely, here was proof enough for anyone who knew the Master intimately. What more needs to be said for verification of his appearance? Surely there was not a single soul who would lie about it. The Master had come and gone. He made his point with clarity. Many people would believe far less important things with a lot less evidence! Still, Thomas was a holdout.

Probably, by now we are beginning to have a real problem with this fellow. What else did he want and/or need? Well, we have to hand it to him; he was quite specific! Didn't he trust his comrades in the cause of Christ? Does he want to be difficult and like some little obstreperous child? Showing oneself to be an independent thinker is one thing. To challenge the witness of his brothers and sisters in Christ is quite something else. We may be motivated to tell him a thing or two. How dare you call into question such stalwarts as Peter, James, and John? Maybe he was one of those people who wished the resurrection was true but had many misgivings. On the other hand, maybe he was just egotistical.

Is it possible, realistically, to place you and me at the scene those twenty centuries ago? To do that kind of thing takes real effort. We would all like to do that, wouldn't we? Our assumption is that if we could really get back to the first century, things would be clarified and we would understand Thomas much better. Don't count on it! It seems to me about the only thing we can understand and accept is his insistence on complete accuracy by physically touching two places on the Master's body. He was unmovable and the history books remember him as someone who not only demanded proof but one who would become a prototype for all of us. Is there anyone you know who hasn't heard of "doubting Thomas"?

Thomas kept his end of the bargain and did not argue. We may not accept this in glowingly positive terms. In fact, this may be more of a deal with God than anything else! We all know or have heard of those stories. Maybe it was during a war and we promised God that if he would just spare us we would believe and go on to a lifetime of service for Christ. There are many accounts of such experiences coming out of the Second World War. Death was imminent and God was told that if he would just spare us, we would go home and live exemplary Christian lives. Some of those promises bore rich fruits for others. Perhaps that is not quite the same as a doubting Thomas but don't miss the similarity.

In a way, there is a childlike simplicity about Thomas. If you show me the goods, count on my acceptance of his resurrection! We might view him as a small boy who wants to be convinced but isn't. You say you can hit a ball out of the infield, well show me. You say you are good at flying a kite, well show me. There is an innocent quality to it, isn't there? Rather than being, at least, somewhat critical of him, we do well to show him some respect. You and I know the story. Had we been there we might have been a lot more difficult than he was. Even today, after all of the confirmation in people's lives, we can be downright demanding for signs of the genuineness of Christianity.

We all admit, in the privacy of our spiritual lives, it is not very helpful to get into an argument with God. Experience tells us again and again he always wins. Sometimes, however, there is solid progress that comes out of our moanings and groanings, indeed, our lack of gratitude and grace. The Old Testament (Hebrew Scriptures), especially, point to characters thoroughly upset with God, who proceed to tell him off! More relevantly, can we feel free to argue with the one who made us, that is, if we do it respectfully and in a worshipful mood? For many, the answer is, "Yes," isn't it? Maybe the most admirable characteristic of Thomas was that once his needs were met, he was totally sold.

You and I are counseled not to tempt God. To do so puts us in a worse position than being between a rock and a hard place! We are insolent to the point of being blasphemous. But we do not want to be too hard on ourselves. We can get our backs up for the right reasons and be purely motivated — like Thomas — which leads us into a newly discovered intimacy with the Father, Son, and Holy Spirit. Never underestimate the patience and mercy of God! While we may have communicated that our man is tempting God and we wonder how he got by with it, is that truly the case? We may not all agree about the answer. But keep in mind, as the text later shows, our Lord has a very important point to make for posterity and we are greatly helped by it. How like our Lord to show us the way!

Thomas was confronted by Jesus. After the Lord spoke, again, his words of peace, he directly addressed Thomas. This doubting fellow was on the hot seat! There, before his brothers and sisters, the Lord dealt with the situation. Let's use all of our ingenuity and imagination to bring the moment into focus. The risen Christ was looking at him with those loving and yet piercing eyes. They are eyes that do not miss the least little thing! One wonders if Thomas had the spiritual stamina to look into them more than an instant. More decisively, could you and I hold up under such pressure? We might be tempted to run but where would we go?

We do well to pursue the matter of Jesus' presence and our reaction. Not likely have many of us had an experience close to that of Thomas. That is not as relevant and timely as our understanding that the Lord comes to us and spiritually shows us his nail prints and wounded side. It is closely akin to the reception of the body and blood of our crucified Savior during Holy Communion. He comes to us in those simple and plain elements. He has done so for centuries to countless millions, many on a regular Sunday basis and some on a daily encounter. In a way, the celebration of the Lord's Supper is a divine and holy confrontation. In effect, he says to us — indeed pleads with us — to receive him and enjoy the blessed event prepared for us.

Is our response to the Lord comparable to that of Thomas? As his body and blood are lovingly placed before us, what is our response? Recall our doubting friend exclaiming, "My Lord and my God!" Protestants have yet to come to terms in any far reaching way with the sacrament many call the Eucharist or thanksgiving. However, we should joyfully give thanks for the progress we have witnessed in the last thirty years. Increasingly, some of us are discovering something very similar to a blessed and assuredly precious confrontation. It is certainly not one of being hateful and seeking negative domination. It is one of invitation to abundant life with potentiality well beyond anything we can plan or orchestrate.

In a world that has become decidedly multicultural and religious, only the real thing shall see us through to victory, now and forevermore! In our nation, long considered a Christian nation, our way of life is becoming more and more altered — in some cases, radically so. Some thinkers, even theologians, tell us we were never a Christian nation. That may very well be true but try to communicate that to any number of people! The perception of being a new Israel with God's special blessing is alive and well. Doubtless we have been blessed and chosen but a new day calls for a new orientation to the realities of other religions, especially Islam. Regardless, Jesus Christ is always faithful to his people.

Thomas is to be commended but not imitated. Intriguingly, our Lord pays him a kind of backhanded or indirect compliment. It is as though he is saying *you are right* and *that's good you believe, but is it solely because you have seen me.* Is it because you touched the nail prints and my seriously injured side? If I had not come to you in person, what would you have done? In fact, what makes you think you are so special in requiring evidence the others didn't? Possibly we are depicting Thomas in terms never intended but one cannot help posing questions that appear to be much in order. It is well to remember Christ knew the future and he didn't.

You did a good thing, Thomas, but the days — indeed, centuries — will not bode well for those who demand proof in a certain way in order to believe the unrivaled story of salvation, delivered once and for all by Jesus the Christ. There we have it! We commend you friend but it is not the way of the future. Millions — even billions — of human beings will come and go. Precious few will have the high honor accorded to you. For the vast majority the Holy Spirit will carry the day and spiritual presence shall be the accepted means of conversion, leading to supernatural confidence and wholesome contribution. Praises be to the resurrected Lord Jesus, who neither forsakes nor leaves his people.

Don't be like Thomas and require of the Lord a specific sign! Our Savior is crystal clear that "blessed are those who have not seen and yet have come to believe." There is not much subtlety here! We honor and appreciate his likes but don't imitate him. The eyes of faith must prevail as the Father works and weaves his ways and will among precious people. What a glorious history it is, as you and I are recipients of the greatest story ever told. We are to see with spiritual vision. In the long run it is invariably superior to any other type of eyesight. Give thanks for the means of knowing Jesus Christ as Savior and Lord.

There seems always to be a significant place for a word of caution. In brief, don't slip back into a mode of requiring the Holy Spirit to speak to you in a certain way. Be reminded the Holy Spirit blows whenever and wherever he chooses. We might also add to whomever, whatever, and however! How supremely happy we ought to be and wondrously we should celebrate the Father's goodness. Seek the Lord day or night and in any place. Listen to the one who has a word of inspiration for you. Learn to cultivate and use any tool for spiritual growth provided. Be resilient to the methods and tools provided. Thomas, we love you and grant you honor. But you had your way and we have been given ours. He lives, Christ Jesus lives today!

Our text is the story of a man who refused to believe in Jesus' resurrection, unless the Lord appeared and provided proof. Furthermore, both his hands and side must be touched. We smile and sometimes wonder why our Lord went so far as to accommodate his demand. After all, who demands anything from God Almighty? Perhaps it is a uniquely special way God walks the second mile to reach a doubting child. Whatever the reason(s), we sense it is a teaching moment for all those who would come later. Learn not to demand a miracle in order to believe! Our Lord and God provides his presence in spiritual power and we are to believe.

Have we not all known those who insisted on proof that crushed all doubts? Perchance we know them because we are the guilty parties! A cardinal theological principle is that we are saved or converted by faith. We are given the gift and receive it in faith like children. The first Easter has long passed and Thomas remains a topic of discussion. The heart of the lesson is there for all seekers to accept: We are to believe without physically touching his hands and side. His ongoing spiritual presence is the pearl of great price that gives us hope and direction for times that try our souls and those about us. It is not that so much is expected of us. It is that so little is expected! In the context of repentance and forgiveness simply accept him by faith.

Fish And Sheep

Don't you find this passage filled to overflowing with delightful descriptions? Only in the Gospel of Saint John do we discover such an appealing and even worshipful relationship between Simon Peter and his Savior and Lord. A feast is set before us and its attraction will last a lifetime for all those who profess the Christ.

As usual, the Master relates his will and ways through common and ordinary means. Who didn't know what a fish was? Yes, and who didn't know a sheep when he/she saw one? Additionally, the Psalm 23 was deeply engrained in those who called themselves religious Jews.

To have caught the scene(s) on videotape might be something all of us wished could have happened. Obviously, that didn't happen, at least, as we understand those things. Perhaps in heaven it will be played back to us in all its magnificence but there is no need to wait and see.

We are treated to a sublime and yet down-to-earth story, filled with meaning so profound that we continue to reflect and ponder. How privileged we are! We are more privileged than Abraham, Isaac, and Jacob. Yes, and add to that Moses, David, Isaiah, Jeremiah, and many others.

Peter failed and then succeeded at fishing. For some of us fishing has just never caught on as a pastime. We use our spare time in other diversions. For many it is golf or some other worthwhile activity. For those of us less participant oriented, watching baseball, basketball, football, and racing comes to mind. Perhaps it is best

87

for us to notice then from the beginning, fishing — except for the rich — was a way of making a living and not much of a hobby. In that day and time, most everything had some connection to providing food, clothing, and shelter. Jesus was good at tapping into the fishing business for disciples!

Yes, we discover the Big Fisherman first failing and then succeeding. It seemed like that was the story of his life! The gospels again and again depict him as a bumbling sort of fellow who managed — at first — to botch most everything. Surely, a man who caught fish for a livelihood would have the good sense to try more than one side of the boat. Anyone with solid business skills knows one does not continue to spend time for very long in an area which is not profitable. But just maybe we should not be too hard on Christ's chosen leader. How often do you and I botch promising ventures? Do we need to elaborate further?

It sounds like it was quite a catch of fish. In fact, we are told there were 153 large fish. By today's standards, this may sound small and modest. Yes, and isn't it fascinating the actual number is given? It adds credence to the whole event, doesn't it? There are those who respond that it doesn't make a bit of difference and all that matters is that it was a good fishing trip. It succeeded, despite Peter's usual unintended buffoonery, and proved once again that Christ's favorite fellow was still just that. We might ask: "Why did God's Son continue to be patient with him?" To be honest, we can only conjecture.

He must have been some sight, because you remember he jumped into the water, after the disciple Jesus loved told Peter of the presence of the Lord. It even sounds like the other disciples were doing all the work in bringing the heavily loaded net to shore. This fellow designated as "the Rock" by many was certainly colorful but many, if not most of us, would not have made him first among equals in the college of the twelve apostles! Yet, the gospel story, not just in John but the other three, tells us he and the Lord had a very special relationship. After all, he was the one who recognized Jesus as the Christ. Some might add, in jest, Jesus had to call him to ministry before he went broke in the fishing business!

Peter had a memorable breakfast. The enormous catch was safely ashore. The Lord was waiting on the beach. He had some bread and was cooking fish over a charcoal fire. Jesus invited them to breakfast. Can you and I imagine having breakfast with Jesus? In our society and culture, we might want to visualize some well-to-do fellows, dressed in sport clothes, sitting in a restaurant. Our dear Lord looks much like them, except he has on a clerical collar! They have the works. There are eggs, pancakes, ham, sausage, bacon, toast, coffee, juice, and jelly. Far-fetched and amusing? Well, yes, because it bends the story so far it loses its majesty. It also has pork on their plates!

They all knew it was the Lord. Plates were not passed and he served them, which is significant. Do you get the idea that there is more than tasty fish and wholesome bread at work here? Do you also sense that there's a lot more to it than hungry, seedy fishermen devouring a tasty meal? It has a Eucharistic dimension, doesn't it? In a way, it is a fish story and yet in another it isn't at all. For one thing Jesus, according to the text, already has the table set. Not one of the 153 fish is needed or is it? It is reminiscent of the loaves and the fishes. There is both miracle and mystery at work here. So, as we attempt to decipher the meaning, food from the hands of the Master is put before us.

Man cannot live by bread alone, regardless of its freshness and delicious taste. It is in the spiritual sharing of our gifts that we are nourished and fulfilled. Our blessed Lord was always giving gifts and in doing so challenges us to do the same. His greatest gift is found in his undeniable presence, as the crucified and resurrected Lord, in the Holy Communion. While Peter and the others experience a memorable breakfast, the message is clear. He is the one who feeds us. We do not feed him. He will continue being the Christ, regardless of what we do or do not do. In our case, however, it is what he does for us that enables us to live the Christian life.

To have fellowship with the Master early in the day has long been a staple for those who are serious about living the Christian faith. To begin the day aright with him is to set in motion forces of good for the entire day. Early in the morning our song shall rise to you! When morning guilds the skies, we cry out that Jesus Christ be praised! While Protestants have tended to be more cerebral in their morning devotions, they have begun, at least in some cases, to learn the tremendous stabilizing influence of attending mass on the part of Roman Catholics. To receive his body and blood is to receive holy medicine from the living God! Of course, we can do Bible study, offer prayers of intercession and petition, receive the holy sacrament, and meditate, how thoroughly blessed we are!

Peter was greeted by three questions. It was only after breakfast that the Lord posed his trio of questions to Peter. The blessed event of both material and spiritual food had happened. Jesus had a plan, didn't he? The focus was now on his main man. The fellow whose track record was subject to criticism was now on the spot. We note it was one-on-one, with the others simply watching and listening. It was testing time and Peter was on trial. There are those who say Jesus was doing this grilling to be sure he had chosen the right man to lead his church. Suppose Peter had failed the test. Then, what would have happened? Yes, and how would a failing grade influence the history of the church?

We get the feeling the Lord wanted to have everything in place before he ascended into heaven. So, he kept pressing the issue and Peter must have felt the heat. Three consecutive times the questions were asked. There was no breathing space, so to speak, as the text presented a trilogy which will forever be imprinted in our Christian consciences. Peter was to love his Lord, tend his sheep, and feed his sheep. The recipient of the inquiries seemed to grow weary and, in impatience or hurt feelings, attempted to remind the Lord that he knew everything. It was a classic scene for all our spiritual ancestors and will remain so for all future generations, provided the Lord tarries.

We may want to suggest to Jesus that he take it a little easier on the poor fellow. As a matter of fact, we may even begin to feel sorry for him. Peter, the Lord really isn't angry at you, but he needs to be sure of your love and thorough commitment. Peter, the Christian movement cannot be tripped up by a vacillating attitude that compromises what the Lord has set out to accomplish. Peter, so much is being given to you in responsibility and authority. To fail is not just to fail yourself and the apostles. It is a matter of there being no room for negligence. Souls hang in the balance. Posterity counts on you perhaps like no other human being who was ever born.

In a small, but certainly similar way, we pastors know this holy routine. It is not secular questions and answers, like being interviewed or evaluated for a job in a bank. Some of us in years and even decades still hear our blessed Lord addressing us as a reminder. For the shepherd of the lambs and sheep to fail his/her boss is to set in motion more hurt than any of us can adequately imagine. It is sometimes scary, but necessarily so. Perhaps the hardest thing to understand is that just because the world labels us failures does not mean it is so. We may have to betray the world in order to serve our Master! The ordained ministry at its intended best is never a secular calling to a profession like other professions.

Peter caught a glimpse of his own death. Again, Jesus proceeded in what can be termed a logical progression. The all-important threesome was out of the way. Essential answers had been given. As Peter heard the words drop from his Master's lips, he must have trembled. Would he have to die for his faith? For a man like Peter to be taken where he didn't want to go, potentially was a very hard pill for him to swallow. When it happened, he was to be old and not have any actual say-so. His right of decision would have vanished but, best of all, is that it would glorify God! Some would say it was bad news so the good news could flourish.

While the holy scriptures do not mention the specific way he dies, well-received tradition has a word for us. Apparently, Christians were going through terrifying persecutions in Rome and it came time for Peter to be killed. This tradition said he was to be crucified like numerous others in the usual way. Peter said he was not worthy to die the same as his Master did, so he requested to be crucified head downward. What better way could he glorify God? It sounds like he received his fate with composure and fortitude. There is a certain divine aura about all of this and it makes us weep tears of both sadness and joy. However, as we reflect, joy comes to the forefront and wins.

Jesus' call to Peter to follow him must have been kept heroically in tact. To believe or not to believe in the papacy and the popes with Peter being first, tends to be a moot point for those of us who have sought to follow the ecumenical imperative. Perhaps it is because recent popes like John XXIII and John Paul II have shown us by example they could relate to Catholic and non-Catholic alike. Generally, our affection and respect for them has become a major unifying force for those confessing Jesus Christ as Savior and Lord. Both men were gifts to all of us and their charitable goodness lingers like the aroma of gorgeous flowers sent to us by the angels in heaven. We have witnessed centuries-old prejudices diminish and even die!

As you and I receive this powerfully relevant text into our very souls, we relearn the amazing genius of the holy scriptures. The Lord Jesus Christ tells us the truth and expects us to appropriate it in ways benefiting every life we touch. We walk by faith but, like Saint Peter, we are given a glimpse now and then. Those precious moments are signposts, making our pilgrimages somewhat easier. Our faith, how gloriously precious and indispensable to our well being it is! Stop tending to feel sorry for Peter and celebrate his life and death. His imperfections and betrayals were but stepping-stones for someone who, by the grace of God, finally grew up in Christ.

Simon Peter is the star "attraction." He is pictured again and again as the prime apostle to lead the ancient church. Our dear Lord just would not let loose of him! It is here that some of us reflect on voyages in our spiritual experiences which are best noted as hectic and perhaps earthshaking. But did the Master give up on us? The answer is in a resounding negative. We were not remotely close to what we should have been but the Lord clung tenaciously to us. We are not in the "star" category. Yet we know firsthand the power of Christ's persistence and his ways of spiritual formation. By the very nature of our calling, we pastors are fishermen and shepherds.

Praises be to God the Father through our Lord Jesus Christ we are told to follow him! All human beings at some time in our lives decide to follow someone. Indeed, there are those who change who they will follow a few or several times. Why not settle in with the Master in the early portion of our lives and live spiritually happy the rest of our days? Laity are also capable of being both fishermen and shepherds. Sometimes they are even better at it than those of us duly ordained by our denominations. Never underestimate the powerful love of God. Yes, and when he absolutely refuses to let you go, kneel in gratitude and thank him now and forever. Amen.

So, Are You The Messiah?

History shows that people are invariably looking for Messiahs or Christs. There is that special person who is to come among them and, in a sense, do for them what they cannot do for themselves. Even for years after our Lord arose from the dead and ascended — yes, and still at this moment — people are looking.

Our Jewish friends, in particular, have this long historical record of watching and waiting. There were, and are, many disappointments in all of this yearning. Indeed, before and after Christ there were those who claimed to be the anointed one of God. Again and again dreams and hopes were followed by disasters.

There seems to be something amiss in most everyone, until he or she has settled on the promised extra special one in their lives. Thinkers, pundits, and even theologians write of the apparently unending search for a great figure. It can be agonizing for some and supremely fulfilling for others.

Don't we wish we had full autobiographies from our friends and relatives telling the stories of their quests? Unquestionably, it would be revealing and some might even make the bestseller lists! Pause to ponder the life of a grandfather or grandmother and wonder about their search.

There are those seeking a clearly defined Messiah. We have a job description. Some said loudly in our Lord's time, "You don't fit what we had in mind!" Isn't such a response modern and don't we hear it every day or so? He or she is supposed to look like this. The perimeters are drawn. Anything outside of them will call into question his or her messiahship. What is expected is more or less

95

set in cement. Deviation, even the lightest, will raise the thought that the one in question is merely posing and is not really the person sent by God.

When we move into political and economic philosophies, we experience much the same thing at work as that which occurs in religion. Quickly, communism and socialism appear on our radar screens. Yes, and there is the admission democracy and capitalism can be counted in much the same category. In America, we labor to keep things straight and not make our Lord an advocate of democracy and/or capitalism! It isn't always easy, is it? Sometimes we ask if he actually gave his approval to a specific political or economic philosophy. Furthermore, we are sometimes made uneasy by thoughts that the American way is not necessarily his way.

Some of the Jews were in suspense and obviously could not figure out whether he was the Messiah or not. He did not give them the answers they wanted. Often lurking in the background of such folks was the expectation that he would set out to defeat the despised Romans and restore their sovereignty. Charismatic military might was at the core of what they had formulated not only in their minds but in their hearts, as well. You and I are called upon to be compassionate and patient. There were genuinely good and certainly sincere people involved. It was not a situation nearly as clean-cut as some would have us believe!

On a more human level we discover, at least, some likeness among pastors and parishioners. That pastor is not at all what we expected and solid support will be very hard to come by! We might want to reverse the perspective and hear a pastor lament what is found in the parish! Laity and clergy alike, who are committed to Christ and his church, know the answer. If we never had those difficult moments in the lives of pastors and parishes, how can we expect to be stretched for greater good? It is frequently not an easy pill to swallow. You mean we are to accept and support this pastor, even though he/she doesn't measure up? Only spiritual maturity, especially sincerity and humility, can save the day.

There are those who have missed the signs of messiahship. It was the Feast of the Dedication — Hanukkah, and Jesus was walking in the temple. To be more specific, he was in the portico of

Solomon. There were those who thought it contained some of the remains of Solomon's temple. It is most likely he was being quizzed by an upper echelon of people, who included a generous number of Sadducees. They were prominent politicians. We might best delineate them as those who straddled the fence between their own countrymen and the Roman rulers.

So, the ruling class was pressuring him to make a statement. Would he please call a press conference? Would he level with them and say point-blank that he was the one they sought? The answers and the ways in which he was delivering them were not acceptable. His works are there for all to see. Of course, they probably wanted a private audience with him! Then, the innermost secrets could be shared. After all, they were the ones with the privileged places in the community and deserved to have the truth of God, separate and apart from others! We all know such people, don't we? Don't let the lesser ones know what we have been told and we will support and, above all, guide you.

We are confronted by something of an enigma. Jesus relates to them that they have missed the signs and yet also wants them to know they don't belong to his sheep. He has done works in his Father's name and they do not believe. Apparently, the Lord's understanding of God does not do a thing for them! Can't you imagine someone being that independent with the power brokers? We can only guess at the awful condescension filling the air. Jesus, we know your parents; they were not all that much and here you are trying to be somebody with little or no proof. The most hectic moment must have been at the instant he told them they didn't belong to his sheep!

Let's face it, you and I miss the signs, too. To celebrate and confess Jesus Christ as Savior and Lord is a powerfully inspiring statement. To be open to what the Holy Spirit is saying next may find us unsure and even faithless. Is what is coming across the screen a part of his messiahship? We thought we had this down pat and now we are confused by being urged to move out of our comfort zones. We must go back to the drawing boards and check this out! Indeed, we can be a great deal like the Sadducees and their fellow travelers and not notice. Then, in a repentant attitude we are urged to see and accept our Lord in a more expansive way. Is it painful? Probably. Is it growth producing? Most likely.

There are those who hear his voice and know him. The Messiah's people hear his voice and not only that, they also know him. Apparently the Jewish powerful elite heard his voice but didn't know him. That really hits home, doesn't it? It raises questions we all have heard so well. Across this world of ours, and a lot closer to home, his voice is heard. Those of us who have both heard and know him have probably lost track of the many dear people who admitted hearing but not knowing. The invitations were many and the avoidances or rejections come back to our memories with sadness.

To hear and to know is to follow. Oh, there are exceptions but that is beyond our very limited comprehensions. To know is to desire to follow now and for evermore. Yes, the roads can be bumpy, but to know him keeps us going because he is by our side encouraging us. Just think of it and give thanks: We are his sheep! Are we privileged and part of the elect? That's a loaded question but, as far as we can discern, the answer must be in the affirmative. It is never cause for smugness or anything resembling assurance produced by one's goodness. The grace of the living God has descended upon us. Christ belongs to us and we belong to him. Try to think of something more positive!

When we are in love with Jesus, we have heard his voice and know him. To know him is to love him! As we follow him in that love through the Holy Spirit, a sense of walking and talking with him fills our souls. Successes and failures come and go. Joys and sorrows make their appearances. Pain and pleasure greet us and return another day. High points and low points of spiritual experience are an ongoing adventure. Sing at the top of your voices that Christ has come. How do we know? We know because he lives in us! So, it is an old, old story of Jesus and his love. In countless forms, the ages confirm all that we have said. In a priceless and unbroken chain, Christian soldiers march on!

Our hope is summarized in a few words of the text. Gone are the days of rejection. Gone are the days of uncertainty. Gone are the days of cross-purpose. Gone are the days of empty living and fear of dying. You and I know beyond any shadow of doubt that we didn't earn any part of our salvation. It was a gift of the Father, who sent his Son to us as the Messiah. There is no waiting in suspense. He was and is here and that is that! Even in the face of defeat and sadness, there is still cause for jubilation. Why? Because we know that face will change and ultimate victory is ours. Regardless of how dark the clouds are, they are always lifted. The true, noble, and right emerge in all their glory.

There are those to whom eternal life is granted. This is very plain. He gives us eternal life and we will never perish. The promise is even underlined by indicating no one will snatch us out of his hand. Those cynical of our faith are apt to respond in derision and suggest the Messiah's promise is nothing more than wishful thinking. He/she would add that it is unverifiable and, in fact, cause for something resembling hilarity! Nevertheless, Christians can be a tough lot and that means we are ready to rise in righteous anger and illustrate our reasons for believing what we do. The Holy Spirit, that probably no one imbued with cynicism would concede, provides and abides.

Jesus proclaims that he and the Father are one. This was an outright anathema to those with whom he was conversing in our text. To the powers that be, it meant he was either God or equal with God. No wonder they insisted on his crucifixion. No one could be labeled God, especially outside of their power structure! Time and again we get the idea, unless they can name him the Messiah and give him their approval, he would always be deficient and not measure up. We may find a form of solace in their ways and even a form of comfort but let us look into our mirrors and be honest about our affinities.

Who can begin to define or depict eternal life? Well, we have a few indicators. To be on firm ground and on the safe side, all we truly need to do is accept the fact we are going to spend eternity with the Father, Son, and Holy Spirit. To try to fill in blank spaces with our so-called brilliance may only confuse the very people we are attempting to help. What more do we need to know? We are going to be with God forever, living in bliss and perfection. There will be no end to our flawless and perfect existence. Time will have no bearing. The creator of time will be in charge and no one will be able to remove us from the Father's hand. What else can we seriously ask for?

Some of us have believed virtually all our lives that heaven or eternal life is built into the very fabric of our Christian existence. To be a Christian is to acknowledge and profess the reality of life after death with our blessed Lord. It does not make any sense to us to espouse a religion that says heaven is all right but we can take it or leave it. As we go about our witnessing, there is the firm pledge of heaven. As we pastors preach our sermons and celebrate Holy Communion, there is our Savior's Word that we are scheduled for heaven in due time. The evidence builds and certainty becomes second nature. We probe deeply into our souls and there is no disappointment. Heaven is ours!

It is a time of confrontation. The powers that be are pushing for Jesus to announce he is the Messiah. Jesus is even more determined to let them know that they have been missing the point all along. He has told them, mostly by his miraculous works, but that does not seem to register. In saber-like fashion, he sends a bullet to their breasts, which communicates a fact likely infuriating them: They do not belong to his sheep. The insiders are really the outsiders! Their need to be in control and dominate has left them on the outside looking in. Sometimes this predicament rings a bell about the institutional church, doesn't it?

Our Lord deals with them in candor, filled to overflowing with confidence, and causes their comfort zones to be rudely shaken. You and I find ourselves in circumstances not all that different upon occasion. We plant our feet, confess him as Savior and Lord, and prepare, if need be, to do spiritual battle. We deal with people on a daily basis who are not his sheep. Oh, they have heard his voice but have explained it away — sometimes in clever ways. They don't know him and are not interested in him because he is just not their idea of what a Messiah should be. But, praise God, we follow him in spirit and truth all the way to the pearly gates and he beckons to us to come on in.

Recognizing His Disciples

Recognition of people, places, and things is a fundamental prerequisite of successful living. We count on signs to guide us. Most of us take it for granted. We move through life in various speeds and count on our powers to recognize who and what is about us. It is so simple and pervasive that we hardly notice.

The obvious is with us and yet is it so obvious? Our talents of interpretation and, yes, our prejudices are sometimes awkwardly there for all to see. We can never be quite sure how others will recognize what we do. Quickly, we can come up with example after example calling forth human distinctiveness — even eccentricity.

Even in the close relationships of our families, there are those differences in the ways we see our environment. On most occasions, we can allow for major and perhaps contradictory opinions. Sometimes a teenager will shock us and we react in bewilderment.

Humans must make for fascinating observation by aliens in outer space — that is, those aliens some declare are real and even visit planet earth! Until we can, in fact, prove they exist, maybe we should confine our energies to what we do know for sure.

Jesus was going to his Father. He was to be with his children only somewhat longer and a new sign must come among them. How like Saint John's writings to call us "little children"! It is a beautiful way to say many things. Among them is our dependency. Truthfully, we relate to people both inside and outside our churches who can't fathom the need to be dependent. Their philosophy is to go full speed ahead in daily living and not count on any strength but what can be seen and measured. Their view is one of being fully adult and mostly mature. Dependence is not only guaranteed to make you eventually fail, it is a handle for weaklings.

Isn't it intriguing how we can become so professional and self-sufficient, that our dear Lord appears to bring failure upon us? Of course, not everyone would agree with that! Doesn't God want us to succeed? Well, we are now in some murky water. My experience is that God is apt to do anything to make us grow, but the intended growth includes even greater dependency upon him. Jesus goes to his Father and, in a mysterious way, we sense a dependency on his Father. To be sure, theologians have kept such a topic for ongoing debate. They get into matters of the Trinity and its precedence — if it has one! We need not be baffled because who said the human mind has unlimited capacity?

We can only envision the love the Father has for the Son and vice versa. Maybe a more honest comment is that we pretend, as best as we can. At this interval, we might want to inquire about the relevance of such exploring in light of our discipleship, which most assuredly maintains that we are to love one another. Yes, and candor must rule. You and I can move into those deep waters of gender relationships. For fathers and sons to love one another or for men to love one another may very well produce a situation having great appeal to a certain mind-set. Gender wars are all about us and some are brazenly insistent on proving preconceived male/male or female/female relationships to establish gay/lesbian credibility.

If you and I had the opportunity to return to our fathers, would we do so? Perhaps there is a hiatus and he is deceased. The relationship just never worked out. We wished that were not the case but it is and we don't know what to do about it! Many have known only their mothers as the spiritual strength and voice in the family. Dad is gone. While it is not good riddance — because who would want to say that about one's own father — many have their questions and it has to do with their fathers. Countless men and women have ambivalent feelings. The Father/Son relationship at the spiritual and eternal level interlocked in love is one thing. At the human level it can be a vast wasteland.

Jesus lays before them a new standard for all the world to see. There is a sure sign for all of us to lay our claims, as Christians, before others. It is to be above and beyond everything the world has to offer. You and I may still be at a point in our lives where we accept this new commandment as strictly an ideal. But is that what Christ had in mind? We can talk back in well-phrased rationalizations and indicate Jesus really did not mean what he said in the strictest sense. It is one of those teachings when we say, "He meant well," but the reality is quite different. Therefore, we only attempt to live up to this lofty pattern of living.

In the profane and mundane ways of the world, we are tempted to scale back the highest and best virtue yet known to humankind. We do not ignore it really. We do place it on a shelf no one can reasonably reach. It is just beyond our fingertips as we stand on our tiptoes. Do we like it that way? Well, yes, we do, except for those who understand that Christ does not command us to do something without giving us the strength to do so. Lest we forget, our blessed Lord is conveying his marvelous message to those already within the fold. Not to practice it "within" is not likely to carry much weight "without."

The question always seems to arise in regard to whether we are claiming too much or too little. Some say all things are possible with God and others maintain it is best to go easy and not embarrass oneself! Suppose, for example, you decide to show others your love for someone in your church who has, by all measurements downright and outright, mistreated you. You tell others about the unseemly situation and point to a future moment of reconciliation. The time arrives and the household of faith watches your every movement. You kneel before the person and ask for forgiveness and healing in the context of however he/she experiences the circumstances. The person responds by saying get up and forget about it!

Can we occasionally confuse loving one another, as Christ taught us, with our unspoken need to force someone into an unhealthy plight? In other words, perhaps our practice of Christ's love is truly geared toward showing up the person and establishing our righteousness? Some may exclaim that this is an awful thought! Well, be reminded that we are to be wise as serpents — according to the Lord — and that clear pointer may make us reevaluate our intended testimonial to illustrate his decree. Note the intensity the practice of Christianity can reach! We must count on the spiritual brilliance of the Holy Spirit to provide for us. It is sometimes in our own strength that we want to be and do things that can be hurtful.

Jesus sets the example for loving. His words are without complexity. Just as he has loved us, we are to love one another. We can even reduce this to commonsense teaching — in a sense — in any secular classroom in the country. He points out, "Look, I have done what I am commanding you to do." Isn't it great instruction? You bet it is and we are not left in the dark! Our Savior and Lord is so easy to follow, at times, that we can hardly believe it is him. His eternal brilliance can be lost in our wish that he was a distant law-giver pronouncing theological dogmatic statements. May God be merciful! Lord Jesus, why do we expend time, energy, and intelligence to misunderstand you?

The everlasting benchmark of his love was and is shown in the crucifixion. He laid down, and continues to lay down, his life for his sheep and lambs. It is a sacrificial love, radiating throughout the universe. When the devils and demons of Satan unleash their godless fury in wars and pestilence, we cling to hope in the love shown us. When things are the darkest and all hell is breaking loose, there is the man on a cross praying that the culprits may be forgiven, for they know not what they do. But let us not be one-dimensional. When our affluence and spoiled ways call into question the authenticity of his love, he pleads on his cross for our renewal!

Why is it so hard to get Christians to accept and practice Jesus' example for living? We have been at it for twenty centuries. Many areas of the world, especially the United States and Europe, have promoted the Christian faith. In the USA, we have sought by both theory and practice to make it possible for his teaching to be implemented. True, we had our share of denominational wars and the testing of the church/state relationship. Nevertheless, we must admit that regardless of what measuring device we use, we have fallen woefully short. Maybe it is just too obvious. Maybe we have had it too easy and suspect things will run just as smoothly whether we take our Lord's summons to heart or kick it under the rug for now.

Those of us who seek to be the best we can be wonder about our children and grandchildren. What one characteristic of our lives can we leave with them to enhance their lives? We know the answer is the love of Jesus Christ. Our timidity gets in the way and our lack of depth spirituality exposes us. Our gift is real love and it is evidenced in the example perpetually set before us in the holy scriptures and is given life by the Holy Spirit. Some of us are so good to our grandchildren. To ask from us is to grant almost instantaneously their request. Do we spoil them? Most of us know that answer. Just maybe they catch more of the love of Christ in us than we know.

Jesus gives us our trademark. If we have his love for one another, everyone will know we are his disciples. That is our trademark. It isn't the great preachers of yesteryear and today. It isn't memorizing the creeds. It isn't giving our money to our churches in record numbers. It isn't putting up concrete memorials, so we will be properly remembered and appreciated. Again, we are driven to admit that it is a way of life filled with love for one another, especially within the household of faith. Our Lord's love practiced in the churches always has a way of moving beyond the walls, so the world can experience our trademark.

When we begin to grow old, we sense the Lord is still pleading for us to love one another, so the world will know we are his disciples, and it seems to become more preciously piercing. It is his way of letting us know he has not given up on his children. The message is the same. We cannot alter it and he refuses to grant an abridgement. The Christ of the ages keeps right on insisting in loving firmness. Long after we are gone, it will be the same. The forms that try to contain our religion will change and often succeed. The indispensable heart of the gospel — to love one another so others will know we are his followers — will absolutely not change.

Human proclivities, being what they are, would very much like to soften or even relegate the trademark to a secondary place. Why can't we just create categories and point to them as the legitimate way to know the power of our faith? For example, those who claim to be saved and sanctified are a category unto themselves where you can always see evidence of his supreme message. Perhaps we could maintain that if we receive the Holy Eucharist every day, we have arrived, and nothing else needs to be mentioned. This love thing, as Jesus puts it, is not only a pesky and feisty command; it is written in indelible ink and refuses to be silenced by the most destructive computer virus!

Once we understand and fully accept that we have a living faith, we are on the way to coming to terms with our Lord's teaching. Saint Paul aids us in the brilliantly written passage of the way of love in 1 Corinthians chapter 13. He interprets, like no one else, his crucified Lord's divine indoctrination. When we are tempted to move the prime message of the ages for Christians over to the sidelines, we are blissfully beckoned to note the trademark that will just not go away. Try as we may, we are defeated by a stubborn and enduring command Christ says belongs to us. We object and evade at our own peril. It is a command we must obey so that others may know to whom we belong.

Both the Father and Son have been glorified. The earliest disciples of two thousand years ago belong to them as children. It is also just as true for you and me right now! A standard has been set in place to be permanent. The body of Christ will seek to practice it among themselves. The world will observe and survey. We hope and pray that our act of loving each other will be a divine program of salesmanship, leading to many conversions. Christ has set the example in stone and it shall neither be moved nor crushed by the forces of evil. Let the fury of hell be unleashed and witness his commandment, showing all its everlasting stability.

For centuries, the world has fixed a skeptical eye on the way it is to recognize his disciples. Sadly, his disciples have been wordy and vague about the reality of loving one another within the body of Christ. You and I have, far too often, sought a diversion or substitute for the actual working out of what he most certainly puts before us for implementation. Let's go watch baseball on television and deal with it some other time! Let's do a lot of Bible study in Psalm and Proverbs and lay aside our Master's lofty decree! Oh, we have our ways, don't we? Perhaps for a time we should remember that we are his "little children" and beg for help.

Keeping His Word

Keeping our word has a long and positive history in our nation. For generations, a man was known by whether or not he kept his word. His word was his bond. Deal after deal was made on that basis. The essentials of the business world found it always helpful and even necessary for commerce to run smoothly.

Some of us can remember vividly how these agreements functioned. Woe be unto that man who did not keep his word! If it happened more than once or twice and there were no extenuating circumstances, he was marked as a bad risk. Our fathers and grandfathers always knew instinctively what was at stake.

Our dear Lord points out to us without fanfare, "Those who love me will keep my word." He adds a whole new dimension to the business transactions, mostly of yesteryear, and the need of keeping one's word. He kept his word and now they (and we) are to keep ours. The prerequisite is love.

We get a firsthand preview into the dynamics of practicing the Christian faith. It sets in motion the way we are equipped to live in a conquering fashion among the foibles of human interactions. We are so blessed!

Our Savior and Lord prepares us for his physical absence. Many of his followers, according to holy scripture, witnessed him living, dying, and resurrected among them. If he would just stay as the risen Lord and minister to them, it would be a miraculous blessing! Don't you imagine there were many who not only wished for this but desperately hoped he would physically stay with them? All of them had already been through so much. Admittedly, not many of them seem to entertain the notion that he would arise from the dead. But he did, so that all would be as it should be.

Some may have begged him to stay. What would you and I have done under those unique circumstances? We can't be sure, of course, but in all likelihood, we would reflect those same desires and yearnings. Jesus, you are going to put us through hell on earth and then you are leaving us! That might be somewhat of a stretch. Yet, knowing human nature, it may be almost exactly some of their thoughts and feelings. Spiritual electricity is in the air and the voltage is impossible to measure. Since John's Gospel is written more in a mystical and devotional fashion, it is hard to perceive the timing of the writing. Of one thing we can be certain, and that is that substantial change is in the air we breathe.

Like none of the other gospels, John keeps reminding them of the very close relationship between Jesus and the Father. It is as though he wants to be certain there is no misunderstanding. Jesus relates carefully that both he and the Father will come to them and make our home with them. He is doing the will of the Father and the Word they hear is not his but that of the Father. Jesus did not come to the earth by his own will, but by the Father, who sent him. So, all the preparation is being done in conjunction with the Father. Perhaps there is no more clear place in the gospels which illustrates the uniqueness of John's writing. However, this should not be a problem because many of us have learned that even the synoptics tell individualized stories!

Soon, Jesus will be gone from their midst. How on earth will they get along without him? It must have been a sad moment drenched with apprehension and uncertainty. If they have on their listening ears, provision is being made for them. Something will come into their lives that may even make them wonder why there was any sadness whatsoever! The key is to love their Lord. Otherwise, they will be unable to keep his Word. The Word was given to the Son by the Father, who has loved all of us from the foundation of the world. It is reminiscent of the twinkling of an eye that seems to contain more — far more — time than can be measured.

Their Savior and Lord reveals the work of the Holy Spirit. The Advocate, the Holy Spirit, is being sent by the Father in the name of the Son. The chief function will be to teach his disciples every-thing. Likewise, they will be reminded of all he has said to them. That is quite a tall order! While this precious Spirit would open the door to untold blessings, the abuse by the unscrupulous would wreak havoc among some of God's people. The purity of inspiration and guidance has been tested more times than anyone can count. Yet, our Lord's message is crystal clear. The Holy Spirit will be their teacher and act as a reminder of all Jesus has said to them.

Some view this promise as the creation of a divine pipeline to the Father and the Son. Through this conduit, the Master will con-tinue to walk and talk with them. Others would even go so far as to call it a dispenser of practical truth for those adhering to the salva-tion of Jesus Christ. However we come at it or which descriptive phrases we use, one thing is sure and definite: They in the first century and all who follow have access to the guidance of our Sav-ior and Lord. The provision has been made. You and I are the re-cipients. We are not neglected children who have to guess how to live our lives. Yet, dear friends, we do have to be receptive!

So much has been given to us. The Holy Spirit abides with us and provides for us. If we trust and obey, we are going to be happy in Jesus! The certainty of the promise is emblazoned in the Word of the living God. We might want to pause for a few minutes and begin to inquire just what more can we need. Our Advocate is per-manently with us. Every day (and night) is a good one, filled with opportunities to serve God and all of humankind that touches our lives. What more can you and I possibly ask? The thrilling close-ness of the Lord is beyond price tag. None of us may be saints or saintly but we know something about the riches of Jesus Christ.

Spiritually, we are only limited by our failure to listen and re-jecting inspired powers of observation. Yes, it is possible to listen to hurting people and deal with intimate problems without gossip-ing! Yes, it is possible to have 20/20 vision and move to provide and/or enable healing to happen! Well, time is wasting, isn't it? We are behind and need to catch up. Our Lord has so many goodies in store for us and we nibble away at some stale carrot cake. Why are you and I so privileged? Well, we didn't earn any of it. It is all a gift from God. The secret is out (and it really wasn't much of one) that his will and ways are at work individually and collectively. Praise God from whom all blessings flow!

Their Savior and Lord leaves them his perfect peace and more. His good-byes are enshrined in the literature of the universe. They are forever relevant to all who would call themselves his disciples. A peace which passes all human understanding is given. It has a purity of purpose and perfection we can only kneel before in grateful expressions. We are in awe and earnestly hope it will descend upon us and never leave us. We learn, however, in our spiritual journey that we cannot contain or control it. Rightfully, like virtually everything the Master gives us, it is, in fact, a gift from God Almighty. Fortunately, for you and me, it is one that keeps on giving and we marvel at its tenacity.

We freely and openly admit that not all who call upon the name of Christ receive his peace that the world cannot give. Some seem to be afflicted at every turn in life. What went wrong? We are not to be judgmental and we are not to play the part of a guru dispensing esoteric wisdom. We are to be sympathetic and pray for the time they, too, will experience what we know in our lives. Truly, it is not because of our superior goodness. It is not because God just doesn't love them. Only the infinitely wise Creator of all has the answers. Let us humbly admit there are times we know little of that peace and we plead for its return. When it returns, how blessed we are!

As far as our hearts being troubled, we know plenty about that, don't we? Anxiety and even agony can smite us for days at a time. We have all wondered why. Some good souls will inquire day and night why this is happening. Again, what unassailable answer can we give? As we set our reason into motion, it is helpful to be reminded that our Lord's communication to us is in the form of a command: "Do not let your hearts be troubled." The clue presented is that you and I have a choice to make. Otherwise, he would have stated it differently. It is in our ballpark and we can choose whether or not to have a troubled heart. How like the Lord to show us that in this case we have freedom of will!

What is to be said about fear? The case is similar, as we notice the "Do not let them be afraid." A fearful heart is also a choice.

Some of us have the tendency to back away from such an understanding and attempt to figure out a way for it to be a gift like peace. Is this splitting hairs and seeking to know how many angels can stand on a pinhead or some such thing? Are we dealing with an almost trivial approach to the matter? Not if we believe in the wording of holy scripture, coming to us by the best translators the world has ever known. Please, however, do not be too hard on those who try to make the choice and seem never to get any place. Our limitations are always with us.

Our Savior and Lord wanted them ready to receive the Advocate. The groundwork was laid for the continuation and perpetuation of his life and teaching. He was confiding in them before he went. His death will not be the end. Even his resurrection will not be the end! The Holy Spirit would bridge the gap between his going to the Father and all future generations. They would not be left, so they have nothing upon which to believe. There would be no chasm. Yes, there would not even be a break in the ministry of the Christ destined from the beginning to come to us. Merely not being physically present will not jeopardize the Jesus movement.

Since they had been counseled to be ready, there should be no crisis in belief. He left nothing undone to maintain that continuity would be manifest to all believers. No one could accuse him of not planning ahead! His successor would be in place and all of the power and unlimited variations are to be enjoyed and enriched by his disciples. Is there thanksgiving in our hearts? If there isn't, there should be. Is there a sense of being at one with the Lord and drinking from his bottomless well of blessings? If there isn't, why not? We are privy to secrets hidden for the ages, as Saint Paul says, and now they have been revealed. For some of us, this is so sobering; we wonder why some have not seen it before. But let us not judge.

So much of this text seems fuzzy for so many people! Only God can know the real reasons for their confusion and hesitation. It is imperative that those who do understand, at least to some extent, not be in any sense condescending or self-righteous. If we are, then we may be met by more than fuzziness. The wrath of God might descend upon our big heads! With the priceless tool of prayer, we are moved to aid our brothers and sisters in understanding what our blessed Lord intended. During prayer time, you and I shall also learn a thing or two. The Lord is so like that. You and I take dear ones to our sacred closets for quiet time in the Holy Spirit and we are taught new avenues of love.

Just to be honest, we would like to live on in our spirits also, wouldn't we? We desire — sometimes intently — for our loved ones through the generations to know us and what we have been about. At funerals, pastors pray that the memories left by the deceased will motivate better living in others. Yes, and some of us who have preached hundreds and even thousands of sermons want just a tidbit now and then to find a place in someone's heart and mind long after we are gone. Does this sound like an unworthy and perhaps unholy competition? Not on your life! For you see, dear friends, what Christians leave really should be a gift from the Holy Spirit.

It is a moment tantalizingly suspended between highly mystical phrasing and rationally stated commands. You and I can be emotionally exhausted by the heavenly strain placed upon us to understand the transition occurring long, long ago. We have had all this accumulation of the history of our faith to put these verses into perspective and some days we scratch our heads in bewilderment! We know to love him is to keep his Word, but then we fumble along, caught attempting to be in two places at the same time. Then, praise God, for some it dawns on them that Jesus has given us the answer in the Advocate or Holy Spirit.

Among the most touching and spiritually charged words in all of holy scripture are found here. We want his peace that the world cannot give! We do not want hearts that are troubled and afraid! If the Holy Spirit working in you and me can deliver all of that, how tremendously happy our lives should be. All of us have seen some evidence of the reality of such happiness from time to time. Oh, there is no perfection in the sense that there are those who are encompassed by these blessings all the time. It is painfully and incessantly an imperfect — even evil — world. Yet, colleagues in the cause of Christ, he has kept his word. It begins with love for him who first loved us. It is solidified by our consecration forever to him.

The Ascension Of Our Lord
Luke 24:44-53

A Good-bye Topping All Others

Those bidding good-bye are around us all of our lives. Sometimes there are almost unbearable feelings and other times merely a shrug of the shoulders. We may sense terrible lostness. Occasionally, it may be a matter of saying under our breaths that it is good riddance. Perhaps most of us have been there and done all of that.

In the case of our dear Lord's ascension, we discover quickly that this is not a usual parting which is common to our experience. There is something very different here! We weren't there, of course, but it is a crucial part of the Lord's progression away from his followers to be with his Father.

Some professing Christians make very little out of this miraculous event. Some duly note it in the liturgical calendar and rather tip their hats. Still others underline it and emphasize it as an integral and necessary component to the gospel story. Fortunately, the latter has become a more prevalent view among many clergy.

We are called to look into this marvelous matter and make it come to life. We want, as nearly as possible, a complete story don't we? Now, our enthusiasm picks up and we look forward to more.

There was summarization to show fulfillment. He was brief — even terse — as he spoke of the Law of Moses, the prophets, and the psalms. Why should there be any dubious thoughts about his ministry? There it is for all to witness, especially his closest followers. From a rich background of his people everything he has done and said should be obvious. If one were to look carefully and

113

with an open mind, there would not be much in the way of surprise. He called upon and commented about the law, prophets, and psalms. It is so hard for some to understand and accept the fact that his teaching is frequently reiteration.

If we could just come to terms in a positive way with our Lord's place in salvation history, how much more content some really good people would be! While Jesus Christ is the focus for us, that doesn't mean he came to us centuries ago separate and apart from other bright lights. Lofty thoughts and feelings are found throughout the Old Testament (Hebrew Scriptures). To believe and practice the New Testament is to acknowledge its dependency on what had gone on before. The entire and complete fabric is magnificent. The slighting of Moses, prophets, and psalms most certainly diminishes our needed understanding of our costly redemption.

It is crucial that we take note of "everything written about me." Otherwise, we can fall into the trap of subtlety separating the two testaments. The New Testament is the primary statement of fulfillment but it gains power and, to some extent, even prestige by carefully using the Hebrew Scriptures. Something new for Jesus invariably means some connection to those beacons who have come before him and who are also historical figures. While our faith has mystery, it likewise has some teachings so transparent we have to labor to misunderstand! Praises be to the living God for the light — often abundant — he grants to us.

There is no wasted space in these closing remarks. He reminds us that he has already spoken about such things. The foundation has been laid and it is time for him to go. On his Father's great board of historical happenings and movements, the schedule says it is just right for him to move into the heavenly realm. His birth, ministry, death, and resurrection are all there for them to see. The often-quoted phrase, "the time has come," indeed has come! The clinging to him no longer fills any purpose. The Holy Spirit will handle all their needs. The period of blissful and loving power is not gone, it merely begins to take on another form that will benefit all the world. Dejection is not at all appropriate. Thanksgiving is in order.

114

There is highlighting of his crucifixion and resurrection. Isn't it truly amazing how these two fit together in such a way that they are interlocked in one revelation of truth? While you and I separate them as two distinctly different incidents, they are one and the same powerful message. In the past, many Protestants have said Roman Catholics made entirely too much of the crucifixion and too little of the resurrection. Yes, and Roman Catholics maintained many Protestants made too much of the resurrection and mainly ignored the crucifixion. From ecumenical observations that appears to have changed for the good!

The Messiah is "to suffer" (crucifixion) and "to rise from the dead" (resurrection). As he prepares to ascend, our Lord does not deal with them by dividing the events. To have one is to have the other. Aren't we blessed and, in a way, relieved by this? As we reflect, how else can we have the doctrine and practical power to live out our faith? We would assuredly hate to attempt to live by the teachings of a dead Messiah. Why not live by Socrates, Plato, Aristotle, or some great philosopher? While we may be tempted to live in the basking light of him arising from the dead, how can we defend a salvation devoid of supreme sacrifice? Again, we detect it is not either/or but both/and.

Some would call it a trite reminder, but, it is nevertheless true the two provide us with the core belief absolutely necessary to the legitimacy of the Christian religion. Diminish one or the other and be prepared to deal with a religion weakened, weary, and worrisome. Who can defend a diminished doctrine devoid of earthly and heavenly power? There is a supernatural characteristic to our faith, which is simply a nonnegotiable. Much to the chagrin of some well-meaning people, they learn that the way to eternal life is found only in the twin towers of which we are speaking. Experience and history point out to you and me that the need to transcend orthodox belief can be very dangerous!

In the Christian context to love one another and to do unto others what we would have them do unto us is an ethical dilemma, unless we have accepted both cross and the crown. In reality to love the Lord our God with our whole heart, mind, soul, and strength and our neighbors as ourselves is a natural fruition of the two. The ideal of pre-Christian teaching becomes reality with the power the two give us. Are we seeking to be too theological for our Lord's sheep and lambs? Not if we are totally serious about living a victorious Christian life! So, we are gently but sometimes firmly summoned to believe what our precious Master tells us to believe. Basic doctrine always does make a big difference in the way we go about being disciples of Christ.

There was proclamation of repentance and forgiveness of sins to go in his name to all nations, but it was to begin from Jerusalem. The Gentiles were to have full access, but it was to begin from the holy city of Jerusalem. In a way, these words helped us to stay honest. It was not to begin at Rome, Constantinople, New York City, or Nashville, Tennessee! At first, our dear Lord came to his own people. He ministered mostly to them. Paul, Peter, John, and others would take it eventually to every part of the world. Is it any wonder that sometimes our Jewish friends look at us in disbelief? Just maybe they are trying to convey to us that we have forgotten our roots. Yes, it behooves us to read the holy scriptures carefully.

Please note that there is no question about our having sins. We deal with them by repenting and receiving forgiveness. This revelation unquestionably does away with those who tell us there isn't such a thing as sins and why don't we just seek better adjustment and accommodation to our environment? Well, yes, such a frame of mind and behavior is all about us. Some of our best and brightest people do some of the best and brightest misleading! But let us be patient and compassionate. We are obligated, at least, for a time to hear what they have to say. The only perfection you and I can claim is most certainly found in our willingness to repent and receive forgiveness. There is cause to pause and give thanks.

Deeply ingrained in the fall of humankind is the penetrating reality that we are not what we were originally intended to be. However we tell the story or create the narrative, the fact of our being much less than our Creator intended is omnipresent. In his undying love, Christ preaches and teaches this to all of us. He gives us a peek at what we are intended by his healing, especially spiritual restoration. He provides a way out of our hopelessness and helplessness by the graces of repenting of our sins and receiving his forgiveness. By extension we are moved into human interaction and apply these graces. To move away from our escape hatch is to delay the essential and perhaps to push us to the edge of hell.

Those in the first century and in the twenty-first century, plus all in between, are validators. As we look at ourselves and observe others in spiritually sensitized ways, our plight is ever with us. But let us not be downcast; after all, our glorious and satisfying getaway is also with us. Thus, sayeth the Lord! Knowing and thoroughly believing this ought to make us humble, sincere, and confident in the Lord. Daily confession of our sins of omission and commission is nothing more than good common Christian sense. A warm heart and willing spirit that is open to granting forgiveness to our comrades is nothing more than a reasonable expectation. The long-suffering Christ paid the price and continues to pay it from his heavenly throne.

There was confirmation that we were witnesses. We are led through his concise statement and then taken as far as Bethany, near the Mount of Olives, about two miles east of Jerusalem. His Word was spread among them and hopefully heard by most of his disciples. Soon they would receive power from on high. After all was prepared, the ascension occurred. Those who were present at these singular events and one-of-a-kind experiences were privileged in ways we have difficulty describing. Were all of his followers there? Not likely, and probably no chance whatsoever. Some activists might even want to shout the unfairness of it all!

With lifted hands, he blessed them and was carried into heaven. That miracle of the moment is one many of us would like to have attended. That's a healthy response and it should never provoke the slightest twang of envy. Once in a while, we run across people who say that if they had only been there, they would be able to believe. As we search our souls, maybe we discover a hiding part that wants the proof of a miracle before believing. If we could have been eyewitnesses, all doubt would be gone! Who are we trying to deceive? Remember Jesus fulfilled the need of doubting Thomas, but he called those blessed who have not seen but believe. Faith given to us by the grace of God and buttressed by much prayer and serious Bible study carries the day for most of us.

117

The ascending scene calls forth worship of him and a return to Jerusalem with great joy. So, our Lord puts the finishing touches to his ministry by an ascension which was unparalleled. In innumerable ways artists have tried to capture the momentous occurrence. It's fair to admit accuracy in all details will have to await another day and time. There are no living witnesses among us, but why should there be? They were told, and we as well, that the Holy Spirit would come to fill the bill. You and I are witnesses to that Spirit. Day after day we are reminded gently and at times harshly to be ever growing in the grace of our Savior and Lord, Jesus Christ.

After all had taken place, the disciples were found continually in the temple blessing God. It would not be possible for us to measure the intensity of those gatherings. It is not at all necessary for us to attempt to do so. What is necessary is for us to plead with our God this glorious episode be imprinted in us forever. We can appreciate it only with spiritual eyes and ears. But we can do that, so let us not feel slighted CNN or some other news media didn't take us there! All the disciples present on that day must have become incurable optimists. They were sons and daughters of the Father. His Son had been among them. An even more powerful outpouring of the Holy Spirit was at hand. It was a day like no other and the Father has not seen the need to repeat it.

We become aware quickly that Jesus places before us a concise statement. It is as though the heavy work is done and only a summarizing reminder is needed. So much is said in so little space. His threefold ministry of preaching, teaching, and healing has been accomplished. His holy sacrifice has been received by the Father and his resplendent resurrection is a matter of record. All are inscribed here below and in heavenly places. The essence of victorious living is in the gift of repentance and forgiveness. An outpouring of the Holy Spirit is only a brief time away. Yes, and with hands so preciously beautiful lifted, he was gone, leaving them with joy — mostly unspeakable!

Are you and I able to believe wholeheartedly everything that has happened? Are we then able to be radiant witnesses on behalf of Christ and the church? Herein, in these questions and their answers, lies the real conclusion. We are inspired to live out the revelation and pass it on to others. What a remarkably and truly wonderful job we have! It is our primary vocation in this life, whether we are clergy or laity. We are to be held accountable. If there is some fear in that, so be it. It is only a way of communicating the truth found in the holy gospel. There is a clarion call to give thanks and seek to be all we are asked to be by the Christ, no more and no less.

Call To Oneness

When, dear God, shall Christians all be one? It is a first-century inquiry. It is a here-and-now recurring question. Countless programs have been launched. Numerous proposals have been given. Only God knows how many problems have risen in our quest for Christian unity.

We live and minister in the twenty-first century in ways not that different from what our spiritual ancestors experienced. Have some things and relationships improved, especially since Vatican II? The answer without doubt is a resounding, "Yes" but, as we applaud, we are caught by recognizing that much has yet to come into place.

Chapter 17 of the Gospel of John or Jesus' "High priestly prayer" still calls out to you and me. The verses under consideration speak with majestic authority and demand to be heard until all precious parts of the puzzle fall into place. At times, the Holy Spirit grieves and groans in sorrow.

Our stance must always be never, never to give up. The world has been watching a long, long time and it continues to watch. Some of us yearn in nearly perpetual pain for the great day of days. We know it is to be but we do not know the final configuration. We must be patient.

The Father and Son are perfectly related in love. This is such a lofty idea and what are we to do with it? Perhaps our response is that God is God and there is no reason to take it as spiritual fact but more like a mystical moment that is unique to John's Gospel. In other words, any serious understanding is not necessary for the living out of practical matters in the Christian faith. If we do, we have missed truth intended for us and given in the holy scriptures as supreme revelation. After all, there were many writings competing to be in the New Testament and this gospel made it!

Love of this variety is so pure and noteworthy it tends at times to boggle the imagination of those claiming to be in a relationship with Jesus Christ. How do we attempt to understand in an elementary respect our quandary? We beg for our wills to have superimposed upon them the will of the Father. We may never have a rational understanding which satisfies us. It helps immensely to know there is a peace that passes all understanding. We enter another level of spirituality and begin to be gripped by the powerful love the Father has for the Son and vice versa. By way of a footnote, we must not allow our difficulties to tempt us into defeat.

The loving Father goes through the agony of the loving Son being killed like a common criminal and made even worse because of the indescribable humiliation for everyone present to view. The bond of love would not and could not break! Even a sense of being forsaken would offer only a brief look into the humanity of Jesus. If he were truly human, how could it possibly be any other way? Certainly one of the essentials of our faith is the acceptance that in order for our Savior and Lord to be powerfully valid he had to be fully a human being. The centuries-old problem of him just going through the motions — if it were true — would extremely diminish our religion. The supreme sacrificial lamb would be the Son of the Father!

Is our call to oneness one which self-destructs because many in our world see us as worshiping two gods? Our Jewish and Muslim friends have always had a problem with such mathematics. How can one plus one equal one? Perhaps we are straining to solve a problem which eludes solution. However, when we really allow our intellect to function under the guidance of the Holy Spirit, a blessed event is given birth. With God all things are possible. God chooses to come to us as Father and Son, perfectly related in love, with the Holy Spirit. They are one, united in love, that the most heinous satanic forces cannot destroy. Calvary proved it once and for all. As sons and daughters, we are to believe innocently and completely.

The Father and Son provide the model for disciples. The Father and Son are one. It only follows that disciples are to be one with each other. As they give evidence to the world, the world will know the Father has sent the Son to redeem it. It is a matter of depth and undisputed quality, isn't it? You and I can become very uncomfortable. It is to our advantage to keep at the task of synchronizing our wills with that of the Father. Love is in the air we breathe and it is intended to be so thrilling and satisfying that you and I are one, just as the Father and Son. We are not left without instruction and an inspirational sense of our expected pattern of living (and dying).

Those of us who have spent our entire ministries laboring on the behalf of Christian unity, accept the fact no amount of arranging and rearranging can bring about what Christ implores. The latest plan to bring churches together in an organizational framework in the long run may not model in love what we say we are about! Political tugs-of-war to see who controls what may break our hearts. However, we learn we are successful in our quest, as long as we do not lose sight of the vision and give up. The Holy Spirit gently reminds us to celebrate the oneness in love which already exists. It may be viewed as partial, but at least, it is that!

We are never defeated in our mandate, as long as we refuse to surrender. Love shall continue to abide, as we are open to configurations the Holy Spirit makes available. The leap from who and what we are to Christ's yearning victory remains in our midst but even that not so blissful predicament is accentuated by love! We must never dare to ask the practicality of being one on the Father and Son's terms. If we do that, it is like a growing subterfuge, awaiting the time to be expedited by the devil. Love will earnestly seek to save us and point to new avenues of growth on our becoming one. Yes, all that you and I are considering is serious business!

Holy Spirit, teach us to love one another in the model given to us. We are not so much afraid, as we are timid and distrustful. Take away our denominations — if he pleases. Allow us to fail if this is the road to full unity. Bring membership losses upon us — if it is a

123

means for your will to be done. Call down fire from heaven — if this is the only phenomenon for your ways to prevail. Please, teach us to seize each and every opportunity to make for better spiritual relationships among us. We yield ourselves not out of exhaustion and despair, but because we seek to do right and to be right. Reassure us of your ongoing and undying love. We celebrate your holy presence among us!

The Father and the Son convey love with no beginning or ending. Even to make an attempt to speak of love "before the foundation of the world" is a very tall order! Nevertheless, our text tells us that is true of the Father/Son relationship. It moves us away from both the creation story and interpreting their relationship in the context solely of power. Creation and power are favorite tools philosophers and some theologians use to explain God's will and ways. John's Gospel wants you and me to know and believe that the eternal and everlasting link between Father and Son is love. It is a love that makes them one.

Christ earnestly seeks his followers to share in his glory and love. They were given to him by his Father. If you and I can be, at least, something like the relationship described, we enter a oneness that provides unlimited possibilities for Christian unity. Our personal identity is not obliterated. Indeed, Jesus and his Father are one but they remain separate and distinct. Perhaps this is much like a marriage of interdependence in place of either dependence or independence. We are one because both parties desire it be that way! Our faith is truly amazing and we don't realize it, until we grow far enough to deal with the issue at hand. Centuries have impressed upon us that love is the right way to go, now and forever.

So much love spills gloriously into the hereafter. Because of love, heaven becomes a realistic expectation. Simply to live indefinitely without that bond conjures up visions of boredom and lack of spiritual vitality. To live forever and flounder around the universe doesn't strike me as much of a way to be happy! Rule out the heavenly existence thoroughly imbued with love and what do you have? The key to our blissfulness is found in love, isn't it? This eternal virtue brings with it a solidarity. Every thing and every one becomes as they were intended. We were originally made for heavenly perfection and we are not to back away in stubborn resignation.

When we tell the old, old story of Jesus and his love, we are also telling the story of the Father's love. It will be our theme in glory. We will be living in loving holiness and wholeness. In the meantime, we are to be faithful not just in a military sense but in a loving style of living. The intent is clear for this world and the one beyond. We are to be one in the Lord and one with one another. All of our aspirations seem to come together and we praise his name now and forevermore. Glory be to the Father, the Son, and the Holy Spirit. As it was in the beginning and prior to the beginning, is now, and ever shall be. The new commandment to love one another reflects an ever-existing bond between Father and Son.

The Father and Son instill love into Christ's holy church. It is always of the variety that seeks to unite and not divide. The only exception may be division which precedes a greater and more complete union. Sometimes denominationalism has its problems solved by dissolving! Who said the United Methodists, American Baptists, Disciples of Christ, Episcopalians, and others should continue indefinitely for the body of Christ to survive and grow? Could it be that love has its way by providing dissolution and wrecking crews? Experience has a way of showing us that the Holy Spirit can save us for better days by freeing us from institutions which bear little fruit.

For centuries, we have had dreamers point to the most complete configurations of the church, as it should exist in the world in which you and I live. We might quickly add that most, if not all, have been disappointed. The inspirational adjectives from what is popularly known as the Nicene Creed may be a major exception: "one, holy, catholic, apostolic." But aren't we astonished specifically that it makes no mention of love? Maybe we ought to send it back to the church fathers for review and possible editing! Perhaps there is room someplace for John 3:16. We can be certain whatever final form it takes, love will play a prominent part. The church devoid of love cannot be the church of Jesus Christ.

The call to oneness remains certain but the time for it to happen appears as elusive as ever. We may be assured the Holy Spirit is at work, coaxing and cajoling, or should we simply say inspirationally wooing? We may also be assured we will not be telling the Holy Spirit what to do and what not to do. As we have traveled the road of ecumenicity, hopefully we have learned that. If some have not, maybe that is why they become so disappointed and defeated. In a few cases, some of us can point out disillusionment. But let us not be downcast and doubt our God's Word to us! With chins up and head high we put failed attempts behind us and proceed to ask for more love and patience.

Every way you and I turn, love always is the answer. Love in Christ's holy church moves about in ways unknown to you and me. The ministry of ecumenism — perhaps like no other — shows us this. Just when we are ready to throw in the towel, we discover a new and unlikely dialogue is about to take place. Our Father has not forsaken his boys and girls! Our Savior and Lord has not stopped lovingly to be one, as he and the Father are one. The unity of Christ's people, so the world might believe, as an imperative, does not go away. We can avoid, evade, and reject but it absolutely refuses to go away. We are called to be patient and resilient, as the Holy Spirit independently moves about.

A few of us have traveled the country, and fewer still internationally, attending workshops and seminars on behalf of Christian unity. We have given speeches, chaired committees, contributed to dialogues, and written articles. We have been inflamed with passion for the unity of Christ's holy church. Unquestionably, progress has given us increased hope. Love of the Father, Son, and Holy Spirit was, and is, present. As an extension of divine love, we have sought to practice ecumenical discipleship. Our failures are there for others to view but so are our successes! We continue to pay a price for this discipleship but we do so in love for the Father and the Son. The Holy Spirit does not cease working.

As a backdrop of the unity for all Christians, we look worshipfully at the Father/Son relationship and catch a glimpse of what we are to be. While there is an incomplete view and some darkness, we are never left totally in the dark. Human loving persistence alone cannot take us where we are called to go. It can show other Christians and the world we are paying a price so that precious people may join us in the call to oneness. The key is the same as it always has been: love. What new tactic shall we use to improve our movement? In most cases the answer is "none." There is an old/new one that, in time, invariably becomes triumphant. It is a four letter word: love.